Side Show

My Life
With Geeks, Freaks
& Vagabonds
in the
Carny Trade

Side Show

My Life
With Geeks, Freaks
& Vagabonds
in the
Carny Trade

By Howard Bone
with Daniel Waldron

Foreword by Teller

Sun Dog Press
Northville, Michigan

SIDE SHOW: My Life with Geeks, Freaks & Vagabonds
in the Carny Trade

Cover design by Dom DiMento

Book design by Judy Berlinski

Cover photograph provided by Circus World Museum, Baraboo, Wisconsin

The publisher wishes to thank Judy Berlinski for her professional help and
guidance in the preparation of this book. Special thanks to the Buggs &
Rudy Discount Corp., Las Vegas, Nevada; Fred Dahlinger Jr.; and Elaine
Lund and the late Robert Lund of the American Museum of Magic.

Also, grateful acknowledgement to David Meyer for various graphics and
valuable advice.

Events described herein really happened. They are true. The people,
although just as real, have been given fictional names.

Library of Congress Cataloging-in-Publication Data

Bone, Howard, 1926-1997.
    Side show : my life with geeks, freaks & vagabonds in the carny trade/
by Howard Bone with Daniel Waldron ; with foreword by Teller.
        p.cm.
    Includes bibliographical references.
    ISBN 0-941543-28-5 (alk. paper)
    1. Bone, Howard, 1926-1997. 2. Circus performers—United States—
Biography. 3. Carnivals—United States. 4. Sideshows —United States. I.
Waldron, Daniel G., 1925- II.
Title
GV1834.72.B66 A3 2001
791.3'5'092—dc21
[B]
                                                                00-066190

Printed in the United States of America   First Edition

To Penn & Teller

who took time to listen to an old side show magician

CONTENTS

FOREWORD BY TELLER

While my partner Penn and I were playing in Springfield, Illinois, some time ago, I visited the place where Abraham Lincoln lived for seventeen years and the Dana-Thomas house, the most complete of Frank Lloyd Wright's Prairie-style homes. But these landmarks are overshadowed in my recollection by the visit we received from Howard Bone.

Bone was bald and had tiny, translucent ears. When he bent his head forward to make a point, he looked rather like a cartoon vulture. His voice was high and thin (he lost half his larynx in a stroke a few years ago), but he was remarkably fit and had the zest for living of a man who has come back from the dead.

Coming back from the dead had been his occupation, as he demonstrated before our very eyes with his performance of "The Man Who Can't Be Hung." After an excruciatingly long tug-of-war by two men pulling as hard as they could on a rope wrapped around Howard's neck, he turned purple and fell down. His assistant quickly loosened the rope. Bone stood up and took a bow. It was a feat he had done for years in his side show exhibition.

Howard told me that during the Second World War, he had been trained in Itto Ryu Jutsu, a form of martial arts that goes back to the ancient Servers, the dreaded Chinese assassins. Officially, he said the Servers ceased to exist 500 years ago. But during wartime extreme measures are sometimes necessary, and Howard claimed to have used his talents in secret assignments. He told me hair-raising stories about some of them.

After Howard's stroke he became listless and depressed. His friends Mike and Carolyn suggested he write a book on a subject he knew backward and forward, side show magic. So he wrote it. It is entitled *Hurry . . . Hurry . . . Hurry!* and gives the real "work" on the side show acts. Some acts he describes are so dangerous, red WARNING paragraphs have been inserted to ward off the unwary.

Howard told me a joke, which haunts a would-be carny like me:

A carny gets to the gates of heaven. Saint Peter says, "Sorry, can't let you in. I don't want this place full of show people." So the carny says, "Don't worry, sir. If you let me in, I'll see to it that no other carnies ever bother you." So Peter okays it.

Now, whenever our hero notices another carny walking up the path toward heaven, he runs out and says, "Howdy, brothers. I hear there's a red one in hell." "Red one" is carny talk for a town where fairs fare well. Well, the minute the carnies hear that, they turn right around and run straight to the inferno.

This goes on for about a hundred years. Then one afternoon Saint Peter notices our carny, carrying a suitcase and sneaking toward the gates. "What are you doing, my boy?"

"Listen, boss," says the carny, "it was real nice of you to let me into heaven, but I'm afraid I just can't stand it. I tell all those carnies there's a red one in hell, and they all believe me and go down there, and not a single one of 'em ever makes it back."

"Now, now, son," Saint Peter says. "That was just a little white lie, to keep the neighborhood up. No need to blame yourself."

"Blame myself? You got it wrong, Pete," the carny says, hurrying eagerly down the path toward hell. "I'm afraid I might have been telling the truth!"

Although I had never questioned Howard's more dramatic autobiographical stories, I confess I had trouble picturing the genteel, soft-spoken, pun-loving Howard as a lethal practitioner of Asian death sciences. So I asked the proprietor of the martial-arts school where Howard practiced if Howard was really a martial-arts buff.

"More that a buff," the man replied. "He's a ninth degree master of Itto Ryu Jutsu. I'm a professional instructor, and he tests me regularly. And—did you notice the tattoo on his leg? The yin-yang with the red center? I've been told that's the mark of the Server."

Now, as Howard might say, it may be, or it may not be. But at that moment the little hairs stood up on the back of my neck, and I felt like the carny in Howard's joke—afraid he might have been telling the truth.

ABOUT HOWARD BONE

*"I always said if you could survive one year doing a sideshow,
you could do anything."*

—Johnny Meah, in *Freak Show*

Howard Bone not only survived one year, he was with it for most of his life.

He was a side show magician, but over the course of some 40 years he was many other things as well. He wrestled the local toughs in "Athletic Shows," labored as a Canvasman putting up and tearing down the tents in which he performed, was a Talker on ballyhoo platforms ("Barker to you," he wrote), sold tickets on the midway, and was an all-around carny hand. He worked in circuses, too. He could fill just about any job in outdoor show business, and did.

At the end, impoverished, broken in health, and estranged from his family, he returned to his Evansville, Indiana, home town and retired to a low rent apartment. But he never truly left The Road. In his mind he was always going to rejoin a carnival, circus, or other traveling attraction in order to live and die among the people and scenes he loved. He never did. He passed away in 1997 at a Veterans Administration Hospital, a place he looked on with scorn and whose staff he considered "quacks."

They must have been long-suffering souls. Howard was not the easiest man in the world to get along with. He had a personality that can best be described as "feisty." All those years of bucking the public, of living hand-to-mouth in a wildly uncertain way of life, all those pummelings he took, all those physical and psychological hard knocks he endured throughout his life—all those things closed in on him at last. His final wish was to be "buried upside down so the world can kiss my ass." Even this cantankerous dream was not to be granted. He was cremated.

But his last years were not ones of unremitting gloom. Soon after he left The Road he was discovered by the American Museum of Magic in Marshall, Michigan, and enjoyed great admiration and affection from its proprietors, Robert and Elaine Lund. He also became a close friend of Penn and Teller, two unique magic showmen who love the side show world. Their friendship was the crowning pride of Howard's life. Teller, a creative wordsmith as well as a peerless magician, wrote him up in *The Atlantic Monthly*, and captured Howard Bone as I think he would want to be remembered.

In a photo he is in his Martial Arts outfit. A thick, strong rope loops around his neck, ready to be pulled tight. He is in the midst of his favorite side show feat, "The Man Who Can't Be Hung." (We all told him it should be "Hanged," but "Hung" it remained; he knew his audiences better than we did). He smiles at us, a curiously seraphic expression for a man about to be done to death. Appropriately, the shot was made out-of-doors, the venue of midways, carnivals, and circuses where Howard spent most of his life.

The effect shown in the picture is much more horrifying than it looks. It is described at length in the chapter entitled "Torture Acts." In his last years he considered it to be his passport to renewed fame and fortune. It was not. Where, after all, could he perform it? Side shows had become old-fashioned.

Side shows, with their geeks, freaks, and sensations, vanished for many reasons. Television, with its sophisticated productions, has brought the world into the humblest household. To see the "strange" you no longer have to go to sweaty tented shows. You can see it every day on your own television set. There are no rubes anymore. That TV has spawned a new kind of gullibility goes without saying. But that is another story.

Just as important as the presence of television is what has happened to our communal sensibilities. Society does not look upon freaks as freaks today. They are the "disadvantaged," the "physically challenged." They are not to be exhibited or even gazed at. The extreme cases are put out of sight into institutions. The rest are left to try to survive in the competitive world of commerce.

Howard Bone never considered himself a writer. He said so time and time again. Yet he authored several published books. One of them, *Hurry...Hurry...Hurry!*, reveals traditional side show methods for such scams as walking on broken glass, climbing sword ladders, creating an "Alligator Boy," and doing side show magic tricks. He wrote others on aspects of the Martial Arts. He was highly skilled in this discipline, an accomplished Black Belt. Eventually he reached the highest rung on the Martial Arts ladder: he became a Master. He was well versed in literature of the Orient and read voraciously in other areas, too.

Howard was a curious blend of self-pride and self-loathing. His letters were full of news that he had started a book about some phase of his life and then torn up the manuscript and thrown it away.

Fortunately, at least one manuscript survives. He called it *To Dance Onstage*. The phrase has nothing to do with dancing or the legitimate theatre. It is a fanciful term used by those who perform on bare platforms in the side show tent. "Talk to you later—I've got to go dance onstage."

What follows draws from that manuscript. It takes us into a rough life, but a life vibrating with the spirit of itchy feet, gypsy souls, and vagabond hearts—hallmarks of itinerant entertainers from the dawn of time.

—Daniel Waldron/Editor

Side Show

My Life
With Geeks, Freaks
& Vagabonds
in the
Carny Trade

STEP RIGHT UP!
❧
ODDITIES
OF THE WORLD

Getting With It

Admissions – 25 cents
Adults & Children Welcome

If you've got carny blood in your veins you'll travel anywhere to join a carnival, no matter how far.

And if you're broke, like I was, you'll do it any way you can—which explains why I hitchhiked from Seattle to Los Angeles.

It was spring and I'd heard of a carnival there. I knew it would be looking for help because World War II was underway and most able-bodied men were in the armed forces. I had been a soldier myself, but had received a disability discharge. I had to show it once, too, when an FBI agent stopped me to ask why I wasn't in uniform. The guy I was with wasn't so lucky. He got hauled away as a draft dodger and I never saw him again.

In L.A. I soon found the carnival and thought I'd give it a look-see. It was morning before they opened for business, and the place was silent and dead. But a couple of carnies showed up and I asked if they could point me to the boss. I hadn't eaten in two days. My stomach was growling. So first they took me to the cookhouse and staked me to breakfast. The eggs may have been rubbery, the toast burnt, and the coffee poisonous, but that breakfast was about the best I ever tasted.

As soon as the lot started coming to life they steered me to the main office. I asked for a job and got one—not doing magic but selling tickets for the Ferris Wheel.

It was the shortest employment on record. I was fired two hours later. Some guy—a man—tried to make a pass at me and I left the ticket box and started swinging.

Hey, I had a lot to learn about life.

My first day on the job and here I was, fired before I'd even gotten started. I still needed work, so thinking I might land something as a magician, I walked up the midway to the side show. I waited for the Talker ("Barker") to finish his bally and asked him who I would see for a job. He took me to his boss— a different man than the Ferris Wheel owner—and no, he didn't need a magician, but he said he would take a chance on me as a ticket seller for the side show. Ticket-selling again!

That's how I met the side show's "Strange People." They fascinated me. Somehow I felt at home with them. Maybe that is why they accepted me and over time showed me the ropes. What I realized was that all of them—fat people, skinny people, deformed people, giants, dwarfs, the whole assemblage shown in gaudy color on the bannerline—all of them were human beings too. They had their favorite foods, love affairs, hatreds, personal problems, and private lives just like you and me.

But still, they are "different"—such as the ordinary-appearing guy who discovered that by manipulating his muscles he could extend his stomach out nearly three feet. He was touted as "The Pneumatic Man" and his act was grotesquely exaggerated on the canvas banner out front. Living, eating, working in all kinds of heat, cold, wind, and rain—and having people staring at you all the time—it's a hard life. Most of the freaks longed for a permanent home of their own, away from the midway. A few even managed to get one. A few, but not many. The pay was low and it went fast.

Nancy the Seal Girl was only about three feet tall. She had been born with arms, legs, and feet stubby enough to resemble the flippers of a seal. But there was nothing wrong with her heart.

Whenever I got lonely or homesick she would talk with me until I felt better again. Sometimes she would ask me to write letters for her. I was amazed at first how educated she was. Not just in general, but about the ins and outs of the side show business as well.

Whenever I could take a minute from my ticket-selling I would go inside the tent and listen to Nancy lecture about herself. I never tired of that. She had a very pleasant voice. The side show was a large one—a true "Ten-in-One"—with "ten complete acts for one price." The Annex made it eleven. The Annex usually featured a near-nude girl or pickled punks. I'll tell you about those later. Nancy's platform was near the Annex, where she was the final regular attraction. The Annex itself was curtained off. It was an extra-cost addition to the acts advertised out front and was called by show people "The Blow-Off."

To entice people to spend their money for the Annex, Nancy had a specific routine. She would leave her small platform and waddle seal-like to the Annex and say: "Now if you'll just follow me behind the curtain, for a small extra price I'll lead you to our Annex act." Then she would go through the curtain and out the back sidewall, leaving someone else to wrangle the Annex crowd.

She would do this, that is, until one evening when she was in a hurry to get to supper. Then Nancy the Seal Girl, my dear friend, my buddy, told the audience:

"If you'll just follow me, we'll go behind the curtain and I'll blow you off."

We laughed about that for days.

Nancy was actually married and had a son. He went to the Korean War and never returned. His name was Michael.

STEP RIGHT UP!

ODDITIES
OF THE WORLD

Geeks

Admissions – 25 cents
Adults & Children Welcome

The Geek Show was separate from the side show and usually located beyond the carnival rides at "the back end." Its tent was about ten by twenty feet in size. Inside we erected a wooden pit. It had high sides and was rectangular—about four by eight feet. We pinned it together with hasps and hinges and 20-penny nails. A show painter decorated the inside panels with pictures of snakes, reptiles, and other creepy things to make a properly scary setting for the Geek himself. The walkway for spectators was raised so they could look down into the pit.

Outside we advertised the show with a big bold banner that read CAPTURED IN THE WILD! It didn't take many people to run the show. No outside bally. Just one person in the ticket box plus an inside talker. On this particular occasion that was me. I usually turned the P.A. volume up to be heard above the din of the rides.

Before the Geek Show opened we dumped snakes into the pit where the Geek would perform.

The Geek in this show is a man named Steve. Steve has already washed up in whatever showerbath is on the grounds, applied his savage-looking face make-up, changed into his scruffy pit wardrobe, and carefully put on his wild wig.

The snakes are all nonpoisonous and completely harmless. If they bite by mistake it will be painful, but no lethal harm will be done. If we don't have snakes we put live chickens into the pit for reasons you will soon see. Steve drops in among the slithering reptiles or cackling chickens. The lighting is tested. The microphone is tested. The ticket seller has his roll of tickets handy and the front sidewall is opened to the public. The Wild Man is ready to go. It is *showtime!*

People on the midway can hear Steve's growling and shrieking impression of a wild man. Some of them buy tickets and gather to look down at the creature. Nobody says a word. Then suddenly the wild man goes into a crouch. What is he going to do? His eyes shift from side to side. He starts to drool and make odd sounds in his throat. Look out! He is hopping and writhing alarmingly. Suddenly he leaps toward the top of the pit near a pretty girl. The onlookers scream. The wild man is about to escape! I grab a sledge hammer and beat on the side of the pit. I yell for the savage to go back.

The uproar draws more ticket buyers in. What is going on? After a minute or two the wild man settles down. His eyes are still wild, though, and he is still drooling. The spectators watch warily. More people buy tickets. But this is just the beginning. They have not yet seen the horrifying sight to come.

After his original build-up, when the onlookers have grown into a crowd, Wild Man Steve begins to shake worse than ever. He thrashes around. The chickens squawk and run crazily in the pit. He goes into an animal-like lunge and grabs one. He holds it up by its legs to show it is real. The chicken is terrified —no wonder! — and starts to make more noise. The wild man thrusts it closer to his body, putting it under one arm. Then, using both hands to hold the chicken tight, he darts it to his mouth and bites off its head.

The audience is horrified. "Oh God! The wild man has bitten off the chicken's head!" "I can't look!" "Aaark—he's drinking blood from the chicken's neck!"

Two people actually pass out. "Someone get a doctor!" But most are thinking "How the hell do I get out of here?!"

I put down my sledge hammer and direct people back into the midway. I announce that we will open again in about ten minutes and urge them to be sure and tell their friends about the terrible wild man they have seen. (As if they needed any coaching!)

The front of the show is closed. Steve, the wild man, spits out the chicken blood and takes a five minute break. He further depletes the bottle of wine he had been drinking before the show. (Get serious. Would you do this sober?)

"Wild Men From Borneo" themselves are fakes. But the chicken action is real. If snakes are used the same routine is followed. From the time the Geek Show opens until closing, word spreads fast. More and more people hear about the wild man, and word of mouth advertising is the best builder of ticket sales. By the time the last show is over Steve is about to pass out. He changes his clothes before this happens and, removing his make-up and wig, struggles into his street duds and looks like anyone else on the midway.

The final day of the carnival is usually a Saturday. The midway is crowded with people. It opens about noon; we do a certain amount of business, but interest in the Geek Show is slacking off. Then, about five o'clock in the afternoon, while it is still daylight, all hell breaks loose.

"He's escaped!"

"Look out!"

"Run for your life!"

THE WILD MAN HAS GOTTEN LOOSE! People shove and push each other to flee from this savage creature who has broken from his pit.

"Out of my way! Help! Get the police!"

Halfway up the midway the wild man runs between the rides. Show people, the police, and even some locals pursue him, trying to catch him. Finally a police officer yells: "Stop or I'll shoot!" He takes out his service revolver and fires.

Bang!

Bang!

Two shots ring out above the tumult of the midway. It takes the police and about four show people to capture the wild man and drag him back to his pit.

The cop who fired the gun assures the crowd the Geek is all right; the shots were only to get his attention and make him halt. Then my cry of "Buy your tickets right here!" is heard again, this time somehow sounding more excited than ever. The crowds surge in.

It is all a put-up job. Money talks. The show owner and the local police have made a deal. The shots were blanks. The cries of terror came from carnival people themselves.

Once, the chase backfired. Wild Man Steve panicked. He was full of wine and, being drunk, was trying to escape the mob of people in dead earnest.

The police officer also panicked and instead of aiming his weapon in the air, fired it right at Steve. To make matters worse, he had forgotten to load it with blanks and he winged Steve in the leg for real.

Steve got a free vacation at the local hospital for a few days. He was to rejoin us on another carnival several days later and several towns away. He never showed up. I don't blame him. Would you?

Years later, the S.P.C.A. finally shut down Geek shows for good—not because of abuse to the hapless human being who played the Geek but to the chickens and snakes.

As for Steve: if you're alive, you still owe me the twenty bucks I loaned you.

I sure could use it.

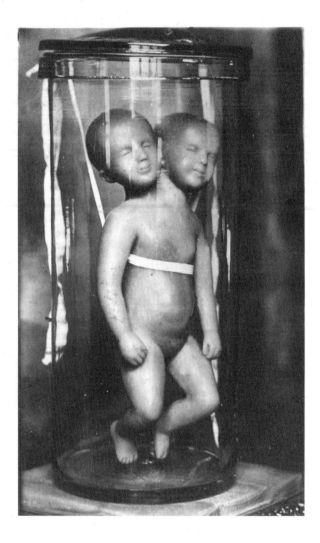

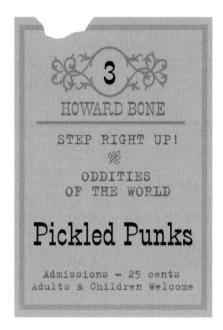

3

HOWARD BONE

STEP RIGHT UP!

ODDITIES
OF THE WORLD

Pickled Punks

Admissions – 25 cents
Adults & Children Welcome

There is a place in Arizona where you can order mummified freaks and pickled punks. A "pickled punk" is a freak baby or a human head in a glass jar.

Are these real? Of course not. They're made of rubber or plastic and look very lifelike—or should I say "deadlike?" All you have to do is add to the glass jars a mixture of water and formaldehyde—the chemical used by undertakers in embalming. The important thing is the smell. That medicinal odor is what makes the display seem real.

A "punk" display makes a great Annex attraction. The big jars sit in a laboratory setting, roped off. A canvas sidewall section hides this from view during the rest of the side show acts. That's because of the extra price you pay to see it. The Annex is never never talked about on the show's front bally. There are not even any banners about it. "The Tattooed Man," "The

Electric Chair," "The Fire Eater," "The Seal Girl," and anything else bizarre enough to attract the attention of the crowds— yes, these are big and colorful in the bannerline—but "punks" —no. They're never ballyhooed outside. It's only after the other acts of the "10-in-1" are over, that the spectators inside the tent are invited to see the sensation in the side show Annex—as I said in my Seal Girl account.

I've lectured on many punks and other freaks—such as a shrunken head "from deep inside the Amazon jungle." How about a "mermaid," "the head of Billy the Kid," or a recently uncovered "giant from Cardiff, Wales"? Personally, my favorite is the "shrunken head." It has its lips and eyelids sewn shut, and the back of its head too. It has long jet-black hair. My lecture always included a few known and proven facts about head-shrinkers in the jungles of South America. I would point out that they lived in the area of the Orinoco River and the mighty Amazon. End of facts. The rest of the lecture was pure one-hundred percent hokum.

A shrunken head is not a punk. It is actually a small monkey's head. The lips, eyelids, and fake hair can be sewn by anyone who can use a needle and thread. Of course, you need the right accessories and someone who knows how to do it. Plus a pretty strong stomach.

When I lectured about the "punks" in their glass jars, I'd be as vivid as possible. Some spectators cried or turned their heads away. Really good patter can make people vomit or pass out. I'd nail it down with a challenge: "These are acts of God. Medical science cannot explain them. It has attempted, yet failed! If you don't believe me, bring your own doctor!"

They never did.

Annex attractions can (and do) make a lot of money, and it used to be all gravy. At one time Carnival Owners did not collect any percentage from Annex admissions. So it was a bonanza for the side show operator. That's the way it was when I came in contact with my first punk show in 1945. By the time I left the road, that had all changed. If you have a side show Annex now, you must sign a contract with the Carnival Owner, giving him a certain percentage of what the Annex takes in. To keep you honest, the Owner will probably plant someone among the spectators to check on you. Money. That's what it's all about. If you get caught holding back, or even trying to, you may get one warning from the office. Notice I say "may."

If you get caught again, you can expect about eight or ten of the ride jockeys to show up the next morning to help you get packed, loaded, and out of there. You have been "disqualified." Don't come back! Some years ago, this "help" was enforced with the use of sledge hammer handles and other blunt instruments. True, this didn't happen often. Actually it was rare. But it did happen. In any case, you never got to talk things over after a second infraction. You never knew the Carnival Owner's motivation. Maybe he was punishing you for cheating him. Or maybe . . . just maybe . . . he simply wanted a more profitable back-end show in your spot.

Sometimes the pickled punks were shown as an independent attraction. They'd be in a separate tent about ten by twenty feet. There was no lecturer. Instead, some show owners went to the expense of having a printer make up cards to set in front of the jars, explaining what was inside them. Operating this kind of punk show took only one person, who sold tickets at the entrance.

Money, to repeat, was the name of the game. I soon caught on that if I ever became an Owner, and was looking for attractions that never had to be fed and never expected any pay, "Pickled Punks," "Mermaids," "Shrunken Heads," and the like were the perfect answer.

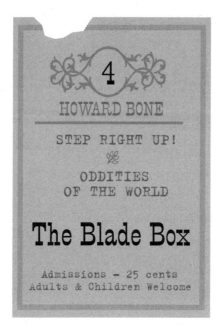

4

HOWARD BONE

STEP RIGHT UP!
❦
ODDITIES
OF THE WORLD

The Blade Box

Admissions - 25 cents
Adults & Children Welcome

The first time I ever did the "Blade Box" was in Boston, Massachusetts, where they were celebrating the Battle of Bunker Hill with parades, fireworks, and a carnival.

The Blade Box is a magic illusion. It's a narrow wooden box that's just long enough for a person to lie down in. The lid is hinged and slotted for the insertion of blades.

"It sits on four legs, folks, (*I would point out,*) so you can see underneath. The victim will now get in and lie down—just like in a coffin. (*The victim does*). I now take these fifteen metal blades . . . made of the finest Damascus steel and sharp as a sword . . . and thrust them down into the box from every direction. (*I do so, viciously*). Notice how they go right through and come out the bottom side!"

The mystery is: how can the person inside possibly survive?

Unlike most magic illusions I did, this one is staged so I do reveal the secret. I reveal it, that is, if you're willing to part with an extra dime or twenty-five cents for the privilege of coming up onto the platform and looking into the box to see how it works. What you see is the person inside, kinked in an incredible position, with the blades every which way around the body. The person has managed to avoid the blades—just barely, but managed. They have caused no injury at all! It's all in the construction of the box.

Usually the person who gets into the box is a good-looking girl—scantily clad, if possible. You'll see why later on. But for some reason, on the day of my Blade Box lecturing debut, we were using a young man about nineteen years old. "George" understood the importance of wardrobe for any type of stage presentation—or maybe it was the side show management that did. He wore green oriental-style pantaloons. He'd even dyed his hair green to match. His well-developed chest and arms were bare.

For some reason, while I built up the introduction, George stood near the edge of the platform—which is important to know. "Come right in close," I said. "You don't want to miss a thing." The crowd—always numerous—thronged right up to the edge of the platform. Several girls pushed to the front. It took a moment, but I realized George was the attraction. He was a friendly guy and laughed and joked with them. One girl kept asking him for a date after the show.

Suddenly, just as I was telling how "this brave young man will get into this box and tempt death itself! . . ." the girl reached up and yanked down his pantaloons. George froze for a second, then whipped up his pantaloons, leaped from the stage, and disappeared under the sidewall. He had worn no underwear. He had been stark naked!

So much for my first go with the Blade Box! Everyone was laughing—even the other side show acts. It took awhile to continue with the rest of our regular show. George never did live this down. But I noticed he stood well back from the edge of the platform after that.

The Blade Box was a big hit wherever we went.

In Canada, I worked it in a side show run by a man whose real name I never did know. ("Just call me 'Speedy.'") We left the U.S.A. at Detroit and drove two days to get to the midway. It would be part of "the Queen's Birthday" celebration. Being a born talker, I made most of the openings on the front bally and inside did magic stunts—including the Blade Box.

This time, one of the prettiest side show girls was the "victim." I said you'd find out why the girl should be "scantily clad." One of the blades would not go freely down. It seemed to catch on something. So I would reach into the box and pull out her bra. Then the blade fell. Another blade would not go through, so I pulled out her panties. This always got great audience reaction. The rest of the blades went through without incident.

"I now invite you to come on stage, up these steps to your right. Walk by the box and look inside to get an eyeful of exactly how she is in there, and then walk down the other set of steps. All this for a small donation of one dime, one tenth of a dollar. If you need change, I'll make it for you. Remember folks, the young lady receives all the money. It all goes to her. (*A lie*). Someone start it off and the rest will follow. Thank you ma'am, thank you sir . . . move right along . . ."

They expected they'd see a naked lady, but of course she was still decent. The panties and bra were extras, planted in the box beforehand.

The crowds at that Queen's Birthday celebration never stopped. Every time we performed the Blade Box I had to recruit two other side show performers to help me handle the throng. Even then, we could hardly control them. We didn't even have time for sandwiches or anything for lunch. Speedy did send someone to bring us coffee and cold drinks. But that was it. As for the money we took in on the Blade Box suckers, I made sure I had it all before my "helpers" went back to their regular acts.

Speedy hadn't paid us since we started—and that was two weeks ago. We did get one meal a day and tobacco money. But no real pay. I had made up my mind that if this was the way he worked I'd leave the carnival and go back to the United States. I'd packed my two suitcases and hidden them in the building across the way where the rest rooms were. But it was getting to be late afternoon, and the crowds still poured in to see the Blade Box. They never stopped. I got no break and my bus was leaving in an hour. It was now or never. I asked one of the other performers to take over so I could use the rest room. I retrieved my hidden suitcases, took a taxi to the bus station, and left Canada forever. Before I departed, I changed all my Canadian money into U.S. funds. It was just over four hundred dollars.

Thinking back through the whole episode, I realized how much I loved what I had seen of Canada. I can still recall the beauty of the land, and how enchanted I felt during that youthful wondrous trip across it. But a circus was playing in Ohio. It would probably pay better than what I was (wasn't) getting from Speedy, so I was determined to find it.

We'd been playing in western Canada. The eastbound bus got me to Sioux Falls, South Dakota, where I was to change for one to Ohio. The long trip tired me. After checking into a cheap hotel and paying in advance, I slept for two days. When I woke up, I asked the proprietor where the nearest cafe was. Going there to eat, I saw on the wall a poster for a county fair in Minnesota. That state was right next door to South Dakota. The circus in Ohio could wait. Maybe the Minnesota fair had a side show where they could use my magic act.

I checked the Greyhound schedule and the price of a one-way ticket.

NEW
BOOK
OF

JOKES, RIDDLES

CARD TRICKS

FUN
MAGIC AND MYSTERY

A big collection of Parlor Magic-Tricks with Cards-Fortune
Telling-Flirtations-Funny Readings-Toasts-Money Making
Secrets-Amusing Experiments-Jokes, Riddles, Conundrums
Parlor Amusements-Puzzles and Problems

OUR

BIG

Entertainer

GYPSY FORTUNE TELLER

PARLOR MAGIC

Printed in U. S. A.

5

HOWARD BONE

STEP RIGHT UP!

ODDITIES
OF THE WORLD

Magic

Admissions — 25 cents
Adults & Children Welcome

M y interest in magic began when I was a kid. I forget how old I was, probably nine or ten, when a traveling magician gave a show at our school—Wheeler School, in Evansville, Indiana. His name didn't matter at the time, so I've forgotten it. But such wonders! Of all the miracles he must have done with silks, flowers, and apparatus, the one that sticks with me is the production of eggs from the mouth of his assistant.

Wow! I would become a magician!

What makes a person go into magic? For me, at least, it was partly escape. My father, I'm sorry to say, beat me up whenever he took the notion—which was painfully often. I still have the scars to prove it. I was too small to fight back so I sought solace in a world he couldn't touch: magic. As I became a teenager there was something else: girls. You don't see many high school football players becoming boy magicians. They already attract girls through their macho physiques. But who'd look at a skinny kid who couldn't make a touchdown if his life depended on it? Magic, with its secrets and impossibilities, gives you the power to command attention by doing something the gridiron Romeos can't.

My first magic show was for the Boy Scout troop I belonged to. You don't think of carnies ever being Boy Scouts, do you? But I was. Everybody has a childhood of some kind, even carnies. A boy in our troop was having a birthday and they wanted to give him a party. They knew I fooled around with magic—I'd borrowed our knot-tying ropes for magic purposes—so why didn't I do a show for entertainment?

I was petrified. I had determined to become a magician. Not only that, I would become *The World's Greatest Magician*. But the prospect of actually getting up in front of people and mystifying them was entirely different from thinking about it. I rehearsed my meager repertoire of card, coin, and rope tricks. In solitude I spoke out loud what I would say during the show. My "patter." That was easy because I was a loquacious kid. (That means my tongue was hung on a swivel!) Yet it all seemed inadequate somehow. As the day approached I began to feel sick. The feeling increased as my mother dropped me off at the church hall where the troop met. "I'm going to throw up," I pleaded. "Take me home."

She refused.

Amazing! The show went over with a bang. I wish I could remember what tricks I did, but I can't. All I remember is the laughter and applause—and one other thing. The boy's father came up to me afterward and gave me three dollars—a fortune in those days.

"Thanks, Howard," he said. "Use this to get some ice cream for your family."

I went home and promptly took to my bed.

But I had discovered there was money in magic, and besides, there was something immensely satisfying in wielding power over an audience.

How did I end up doing magic in side shows?

A roll of the dice. The wheel of fortune. Or, to put it another way, pure accident. I finished high school and was looking for a way to dazzle the world with my magical talents. A friend of a friend of a relative knew of an opening at a local fairgrounds carnival. As it turned out, the job was not for a magician but for a person to work one of the concessions. That was a booth where the mark (customer) tosses a dime. If he can land it on the slippery glass tray he wins a stuffed turtle (of all things!).

I'd told the boss I was looking for work as a magician in a side show. He said he couldn't use a magician and there wasn't a side show within a hundred miles. So I took the concession job. Wasn't it a step in the right direction? I thought so.

About the fourth day the Carnival Owner came over to me and wanted to talk. If I was truly a magician, he said, "Show me." He said he'd put a marked quarter in my change apron and I was to magically spirit it into my pants pocket without his knowledge. He had another fellow with him and they'd made a *hundred dollar bet!* The Owner had bet I couldn't do it. The other fellow, who had seen me practicing coin tricks, bet I could. They stepped away about ten feet and watched me like a hawk.

If you've ever noticed a carnival concessionaire when he's not busy, you've seen how he puts his hands into the pockets of his change apron and jingles the coins. I did this casually as the bettors watched. They had given me ten minutes in which to accomplish the magical transposition so I pretended to be in no hurry. In fact, I even treated myself to a chew. I had once smoked cigarettes. There was one in my mouth when I joined the carnival. They had told me in no uncertain terms to put it out. Cigarettes are a fire hazard around showgrounds. They told me carnies chewed tobacco instead. So, hard as it was to get used to the stuff at first, I took up chewing. It was my baptism in carny ways.

As I jingled the coins with one hand, I reached into my pants pocket with the other and removed my packet of chewing tobacco. I took my chew, then replaced the packet in my pocket, leaned over the edge of the booth, and spit some juice. I let two minutes go by and then motioned for the Owner and his friend to come over. I untied my change apron, laid it on the front counter, and asked the Owner to find the marked quarter. He sorted through all the coins but couldn't find it. He asked the other fellow to do it. Identical result.

I pushed my shirt sleeves high above my elbows. Cautiously, showing an open palm, the back of my hand, and nothing between my fingers, I reached into my right hand trouser pocket. That's where I kept my own money and my chewing tobacco. I removed it all. I spread the coins on the counter. I invited both men to search them. Lo and behold, they found the marked quarter.

"I'll be a son-of-a-bitch!" the Owner exclaimed. But he paid the bettor the hundred dollars. He slicked it off a wad of bills that looked like it would choke a horse, or maybe an elephant.

"Listen," he said to me. "I'll give you the same amount in cash if you show me exactly how the hell you did that!"

Magicians don't usually reveal their secrets. But in this case, I did. (*I won't tell you, the reader—unless, of course, you want to send me a hundred bucks! Let me just say it involves sleight-of-hand and a bit of misdirection*). Before I explained to the Owner, I had one stipulation. In addition to the money, I wanted a statement on carnival stationery that said I was a good magician.

The Carnival Owner cussed me out for being "a pushy gazonie," (which I didn't understand, but later would, as will you) but he agreed. I had already contacted a distant side show and learned they needed the thing I had set out to be—a magician. When the bus left at 2:10 in the middle of the night I was on it. I had money in my pocket, a paper that could help me get a job in magic, and a fresh supply of chewing tobacco.

STEP RIGHT UP!
❀
ODDITIES
OF THE WORLD

More Magic

Admissions — 25 cents
Adults & Children Welcome

My heart fell when I got to the side show and saw the bannerline. The magician pictured on the weathered canvas looked nothing like me. It showed him doing tricks I never performed—a floating lady, doves from a top hat, rabbits leaping out of nowhere, silks wafting through the air—and all from the hands of a suave-looking dude in evening clothes. I didn't have evening clothes. I didn't even own a suit. And I certainly didn't have the live-stock or equipment to do those tricks.

I confessed this to the side show owner, but he didn't seem to care. He hired me on the spot. It seems no magician they'd ever had, had looked like that. They all worked in their shirt-sleeves. They all did simple card and coin tricks, too, not the flamboyant stuff shown on the banner. I soon found out why: big illusion equipment is too bulky for an individual to carry around. We've been called "rolling stones"—and not unjustly. We tend to change employers often. But a deck of cards, a few coins, several colorful silks, and a gimmick or two take up next to no room in a suitcase. In addition, when you are doing a dozen or more shows a day, you don't want to be bothered re-setting complicated apparatus. You depend on your sleight-of-hand skill and your ability with patter.

Whenever they had one, I'd buy a Route Card. The cards cost fifty cents and showed the towns the show was booked to play. I'm looking at an old one right now. I see I've circled the name of a town in Texas. I remember why. That was where the President of Mexico came to the side show. Our boss knew about the visit in advance, and told us to be on our best behavior. He took me aside: absolutely no blue language, dirty jokes, or smart-mouth cracks. Why me? I guess I'd gotten a reputation. I was a high-spirited devil-may-care type by that time, and said and did just about anything to make the audience react.

All kinds of police—state, county, and local, plus federal officers—accompanied the President. A Texas Ranger, two Secret Service agents, and a guy from the F.B.I. had already checked our props, stages, and us. Each of us got a thorough search.

Then: here he was—the President, his translator, and his entourage.

We ran the show as usual, one act at a time, each act in its turn. For my magic act, I had decided to start with the Thumb Tie. I asked the Texas Ranger to bind my thumbs together. That was a mistake. Never let a Texas Ranger tie your thumbs! But painful as it was, I managed to do the magic anyway, catching hoops thrown to me, supposedly passing right through the tied thumbs, and dangling from my arms.

I followed up with card manipulations, producing fans of cards from thin air. I used my own deck of powdered cards. Then I left the stage and went down into the audience. I approached the translator and asked permission for the President to assist me in a card trick. When he knew what was wanted the President nodded his head, smiled, and said "Si." I made a fan of cards and asked the President (through his translator) to select one. "Be sure I don't see it . . . don't tell me the card . . . and please show it to the rest of the party." He did. Then he placed his selection back in the deck. I shuffled the deck—then, using the floating key card (a specially treated card), I quickly found the one he'd chosen. I didn't show it immediately, however. "Sticks" LeRoy had taught me always to miss on the first try. Show the wrong card. I did this—and faked great embarrassment at having missed the Presidential pick.

I started to turn away, then, almost as an after-thought, I turned back. I asked the translator to have His Excellency look inside his left coat pocket. I stood about six feet away. The President reached into his pocket and pulled out the correct card. Great laughter and applause from everyone—except the law enforcement contingent. Before I knew what was happening a Secret Service agent had handcuffed my wrists, and the Texas Ranger was pointing his gun at me. The President quickly told them to let me go. To this day, I don't know why they did it. Did they think I really had magical powers? The President could take a joke. Why couldn't the police? You know the old saying, "May you walk a mile in my shoes." To them I say, "May you walk a mile with a pebble in each of your shoes."

Hey Ranger—that goes for your horse, too!

I told you most side show magicians don't carry heavy illusion equipment with them—and they don't. That doesn't mean you never see such illusions on the midway. You do.

Maybe you see "Spidora," where a living girl seems to have the body of a spider. You know she's real, because you can talk with her as she crouches there in the middle of a gigantic web.

Or maybe you'll see "The Headless Lady"—which is exactly what the name implies. The genuine body of a woman sits before you, headless beyond a doubt, her life dependent on the gurgling tubes that run in and out of her neck.

Or perhaps you'll take in the most audacious illusion of them all, the "Girl to Gorilla." An attractive girl in leopard scanties turns into a big hairy gorilla (or maybe it's just a man in a hairy gorilla suit) before your very eyes.

"GorillaGorillaGorilla!" chants the lecturer. Unlike the Geek, who escaped only once during the run, the monster gorilla breaks from his cage into the tent during each and every performance. The sight of people running screaming from the tent automatically lures others to buy tickets to see what could possibly be so frightful inside.

Then, of course, there are the traditional magic illusion shows, where an attractive assistant may be sawn in half, floated in air, or vanished or produced in any number of ways. But, like the Blade Box, the bulky equipment required for all of these stunts is usually owned and transported by the carnival itself, or by an independent showman contracted to appear with the carnival as a separate attraction.

I was on a magic illusion show at one time. "Jim" was the owner. His wife was the ticket seller. She also—once the crowd was in—was his bewitching costumed assistant. The trouble was, Jim didn't know how to operate the illusions. He knew how they worked, but he didn't know how to present them or what patter to use. He hired me to show him. I did. I opened with my sleight-of-hand act; Jim followed with the illusions. Some of these required help invisibly from backstage. Since we didn't have a real theatre to work in, that meant I'd have to crouch behind the platform out of sight of the audience, to make the onstage magic happen.

"The Levitation," as the "Floating Lady" is known, was one of these. Jim put his exotically costumed wife into a trance (?), placed her on a table and commanded her to "Rise!" That was my cue to work the lifting apparatus from behind the platform. I had to turn a crank. I had to be sure this was smooth and steady, with no jerky stops in midair. When Jim was ready for the descent, I had to turn the crank in the other direction.

I also had one other job. I had to make sure no one sneaked in under the back sidewall canvas of the tent, because we were located at the very edge of the showgrounds.

Once, as I knelt there turning the crank, a towner popped his head under the canvas and started to crawl through. I couldn't shout at him—there was a show going on above—but I was damned if I'd let him in without a ticket.

Part of my magic act had consisted of rope escapes. To loosen the knots after the act was over, I carried a pair of heavy-duty pliers. Without thinking, I reached into my left rear pocket where they were kept and threw them at the intruder. He snapped back out of sight. If you think it's easy to throw something with your left hand while your right hand is busy turning a crank, try it sometime! The pliers missed the man but disappeared outside the canvas sidewall, which dropped down again when he pulled back.

I'd kept an interloper away, but Jim said the Levitation shook so much when I threw the pliers, it was like an earthquake. From that point on, I ignored anyone who lifted the sidewall during an illusion.

The pliers? I never could find them. Someone today has a pair of fine expensive Klein pliers in his tool chest. I had to spend good money to buy another pair. I always carried them with me. Later on, I'll tell you another use besides throwing them at gate-crashers or undoing knots.

HOWARD BONE

STEP RIGHT UP!
❧
ODDITIES
OF THE WORLD

Palisades Park

Admissions — 25 cents
Adults & Children Welcome

P alisades Park may be the high point of my magic career. I worked there as a side show attraction one spring. The side show was located in a real four-wall building right next to the roller coaster—an old-style roller coaster, before monster thrill rides and theme parks were invented.

"Charlie" was the boss, and had a first class side show. He had real freaks with no phony makeup, a "Giant Dwarf Fire Eater," an honest to goodness "Fat Man," and "Bill, the Boy With Two Faces"—Bill had an extremely mobile face and could contort it into different shapes. There was "Alex, the World Champion Sword Swallower," whose bona fides were in the *Guinness Book of World Records*. They were all

".. . real, ALIVE on stage on the inside of the show. See those strange people. If you're in line, you're in time.

Step up, tell the cashier how many, and come on in! Let's go now, while the tickets are specially priced!—every adult gets in to this showing for a *child's* price. Only thirty-five cents . . ."

That money shows you how long ago it was.

In addition to the freaks there was "The Electric Chair," "The Sword Ladder," my old friend "The Blade Box," and others. When I first talked to Charlie, he was mainly interested in who I had worked for and where and when. He was also, of course, interested in what acts I could do. By this time I could do many, as well as handle a range of other side show chores. We came to a mutual agreement: I'd do acts in the show, be the number two talker, and get fifty dollars a week and two percent of the tickets sold when I was on the front bally stage. It was a good proposition for me at the time. Palisades Park was always busy. It drew people from all over the world as well as from the New York-New Jersey area.

Living quarters were in the building where the side show was located. It had been fitted out with residential accommodations. These included a stove and utensils, so we could cook our own meals. And we did—two meals a day prepared at regular hours. We took turns going to the grocery store. If I was on the stage or the bally at mealtimes someone in the quarters would put my meal on "warm" until I had time to eat. It was almost like a circus.

The Park was closed on Mondays for a general cleaning. With constant entertaining and bally, we needed a break too. We always welcomed Mondays for another reason: payday! Charlie paid everyone on Monday mornings. I tried to get my money and be off to the bus stop before 9:00 A.M. New York

City was not then called "The Big Apple" but by whatever name, it was exciting. Vaudeville was not dead yet. If I was lucky I'd see a stage show; if not, go a movie, eat in a classy restaurant, or just see the sights, like Manhattan from the top of the Empire State Building.

Park Management dreamed up special features to lure people to the place. Once, a big-time celebrity—who shall remain nameless, due to subsequent events—made a personal appearance at the Park. I had the bright idea to give both him and us publicity by having him help with a free show we did on the bally platform. This was a magic illusion known as "Escape From the Cross." It was a sure crowd-getter. We'd done it over and over, using one of the bally girls who'd been hired for the inside illusions. She'd be tied to this huge wooden cross at her arms and neck. There were three ropes, each less than two feet in length, and very soft, to prevent rope burns. At a word of command, she'd step away, miraculously loose. The crowd would gasp in wonder, and rush to buy tickets.

The male celebrity was to tie the girl to the cross. This time, she refused. I could see the two of them whispering heatedly back and forth. Then I could hear her spitting profanity. The celebrity finally turned to me and muttered "What's wrong with this drunken broad?" Yes, she was drunk. The celebrity was none too happy, and neither was my boss. We all survived, however, and the incident was soon swallowed up in the endless succession of bally turns.

It was now late May or early June—far enough into the show season for carnivals to have started their yearly rounds. I had begun to get the itchy foot. Something in me didn't like to be in one place too long. Palisades Park was wonderful, but it was rooted in a single spot. I gave Charlie two weeks' notice, checked the Greyhound Bus schedule, and said goodbye to my friends. I didn't say the word "goodbye," of course. I used the trouper's farewell . . . "See you down the road" . . . and I was gone.

Three days later and one thousand miles away, I was in the ring, fighting with a local "tough guy." I had joined an Athletic Show.

I never saw so many blood-thirsty people in my life. They came by the hundreds and thousands. They filled the carnival Athletic Show tent until the canvas actually bulged at the sides. What they wanted to see was bloodshed and they saw it. They cheered lustily as it flowed. After all, it was not theirs—it was mine.

I stepped into the ring with a Nebraska tough guy who outweighed me by a good 40 pounds. I had weighed in at a mere 143, which put me in the "welterweight" class. I had never been in the ring before. I didn't even have a fighter's wardrobe. The show's owner, a man I'll call "Jesse," had given me ring trunks and shoes, and said "I'll try you out tonight. Start easy: one three minute fight. I'll introduce you as a 'Judo Fighter.'" I protested that my martial arts background hadn't included Judo, but he said it didn't matter. (*All these years later, I still don't do Judo*).

The tough guy from Lincoln came at me like a wild man. We were supposed to be fighting by professional wrestling rules, but they didn't exist for him. He grabbed me by the waist of my trunks and spun me to the mat. I was up again like a pogo stick. He punched me in the gut with his fists. He kneed me in the groin. He smashed my head against a ring-post. Blood ran down my forehead and into my eyes. Was I scared? Frightened? Worried?

Is the Pope Catholic? Of course I was scared. I was also mad. I'd had enough of his dirty pool. At two minutes, I tripped him off-balance, applied a martial arts sleeper hold, and pinned him to the mat for the required count of three.

The "referee," by the way, was a friend of his—the local fighter had the right to name his own ring official—and the man hemmed and hawed in his three-count. But it did no good. I'd put the bruiser out. I'd won my first fight.

That's how I entered the troupe of "muscle-head" fighter/wrestlers who traveled from town to town on the carnival Athletic Show. I soon learned to call it by the same name as they did, the "At' Show." Why did I take so enthusiastically to it? Why did I suffer a cracked head, broken fingers, endless bruises, countless cuts, flowing blood? I suppose Mr. Freud and friends would say it had something to do with getting back at my father. But to me, at that time, it was simply a good way to earn a living. The five dollars handed to me after that first fight seemed like great compensation in those days. It would keep me going all week—and in the future I fought (and made money) every day the carnival was in action.

"Fight! Fight! Fight! So where are all you so-called tough guys? You street fighters? You barroom brawlers? Let's find out how tough you really are! Fight! Fight! Fight! Here's your big chance to prove it to your girlfriend, your co-workers, your pals! Fight! Fight! And right now, I'm going to bring out some of our own fighters—right here, on this stage . . ."

That's the talker on the bally platform outside the At' Show tent. He gets attention with an ambulance siren. His loud-speakers are turned up full volume. He draws a tremendous tip. In every crowd there are local roughnecks well-known for their ability to pulverize anyone who gets in their way. They may be ex-Marines, members of a college wrestling team, boxers who've had a few professional fights or anyone at all who answers to the name of "tough." Our talker's aim is to work them up to the point where they'll take on the show's fighters.

The talker brings me out on the bally stage to line up with the other muscle-heads, in full view of the crowd. Each of us steps forward as our name is called, looking as mean and threatening as possible. I'm introduced as "Mr. Judo." The local toughs then pick which one of us they want to fight. I got picked a lot because, with my small build, I looked easy. This continues until we've all been matched and the card for the fight is completed. Then the crush of ticket buyers begins.

Sometimes it's necessary actually to rile the crowd, make potential fighters so angry they'll come forward with a chip on their shoulders. One of my favorite ploys was to wink and flirt with young women in the crowd if they were with husky husbands or boy-friends. These men, naturally, got so mad they'd sign up to "show that arrogant bastard."

One time, a day or two after I'd joined the At' Show, Jesse, the owner, motioned me into the truck where my local opponent had gotten dressed in the shorts and shoes the show provided. I wondered what he wanted.

"You're going to go three rounds," he said to me. "Then 'Norman' here (the local) will bounce you off the ropes. You'll come flying at him. He'll duck and as you bounce back from the opposite ropes, he'll grab you, throw you down, and pin you for the full count. You got that?"

"I'm supposed to *lose the match?*" I couldn't believe my ears.

Jesse nodded. Norman grinned as he handed the owner some greenbacks. It was to be a fixed fight! Jesse saw my hackles rise. I didn't want to lose to this knuckle-head.

"You better follow orders," Jesse threatened. "If you don't, it's a fifty dollar fine!"

The bout went off exactly as scheduled.

Winning, I discovered, was not the only goal. Like everything else on a carnival, it was all a matter of money. If it takes a scam to sell tickets, that's what it takes. You may be a person of conscience in other walks of life, but on a carnival you soon learn to mute that particular part of your brain. We didn't get paid by the hour, the week, or the fight. We got paid a percentage of ticket sales. Win or lose, it didn't matter. The size of the crowd was what counted. The money paid to the owner to throw a fight was shared with us. So we ended up willing to go along with the gag. What the hell? It was only a show, and we felt well paid for our trouble.

But we had to battle furiously anyway, and both in the ring and out of it we had to keep our eyes open.

I remember on another carnival, while we were playing a fair, we had an At' Show boss who wasn't exactly on the level with us. He tried to short-change us. We'd drawn great crowds. People had flocked to buy tickets. What the boss didn't know was that we had kept count of the number sold for each fight. So at the end of the fair, at which time, by the way, he held off paying us until the truck was nearly loaded with tent, poles, pads, and all, he faced eight wrestlers who were in no mood for funny business. They told him right out what he owed. They argued. The boss got furious. "You're fired!—the whole bunch of you! Get off the midway right now!"

I was in the process of loading the last of our suitcases and gear into the truck when this happened. He yelled at me: "That goes for you too!"

"Go to hell!" I retorted. "I'm busy!"

There was dead silence. Then the boss started to laugh. He weighed about 280 pounds and I weighed 143 soaking wet— hardly more than half of what he did. He could have smashed me to pieces. The ridiculousness of it made the other wrestlers begin to chuckle. It was exactly what was needed. The tension dissolved away.

The boss claimed to have miscounted and paid what he owed us. I continued to load the truck, then closed the doors and locked them. Three of us piled into that vehicle and the rest of the fighters went with the boss in his car to the next fair.

Before each match, I would get my opponent and the referee together and recite . . .

— *The fight will be by professional wrestling rules.*
— *No choking, no closed-hand punches, no using elbows, no eye-gouges, and no knees in the groin.*
— *No spitting or biting.*
— *No torture holds.*
— *When the referee says "break" you break. You have three seconds to break or you are disqualified.*
— *If you land on the edge of the ring, you have 10 seconds to get back in.*
— *If you land outside the ring, you have 20 seconds to get back in. If not, you've lost the match. The referee must count out loud.*
— *Two warnings and you are automatically disqualified.*
— *If you're pinned to the floor for a full count of "three" you've lost, and the match is over. Both shoulders must be held down while the ref counts.*
— *If the opponent gives up, the match is over.*
— *You, my opponent, must select a timekeeper with a second hand on his watch.*

Rarely was I in a fight that stuck to all those rules. Many of my opponents, especially in the farm-boy tough-man belt of the country, were rough, mean, and often dirty. They wanted to win—not so much to hurt me as to maintain their reputation in front of their friends—especially their girlfriends. I said "winning" was not the whole point for the At' Show fighters. It wasn't. But we had to win sometimes or interest would fade. And believe me, it wasn't easy. I did my best—won about sixty percent of my fights, as I recall. Many of the ones I lost were the result of "arrangements" having been made with the owner. But when I ran into a smarty who had made no deal and was particularly tough, mean, and dirty, I didn't hold back. I got tougher, meaner, and dirtier than he was.

If the ones who had paid the boss in order to win, stuck to the rules, they got off easy. But if the local tough guy didn't follow the script of the deal he'd made—if he decided to take off on the At' Show fighter and hurt him any way he could—there'd be hell to pay. The At' Show owner would put the meanest, nastiest, dirtiest fighter he had into the ring for the next round, to "educate" the local hero. This was frequently me. We called such a fight a "Tigermatch" and I was known among my fellow fighters as "The Professor." That's because I had "educated" many of these would-be killers. They all graduated from the local hospital with a degree in "Never Again."

Sometimes I even had to "educate" the referee. In one particular episode, my opponent had me in a full Nelson. I managed to throw him, but in the process I dislocated a shoulder. I shouted at the timekeeper to stop the clock. Then I gave my opponent instructions to help pull my shoulder back in place. He did. Time started again. But my opponent decided to take advantage of my injury and started hitting my shoulder area with his fists. I gave him a warning. But his buddy, the ref, told me to shut up and fight. So I did. I used an elbow on the tough guy's jaw. When he screamed it was broken, the referee grabbed me and started throwing punches. I gave him the jaw treatment too. They both went in the same ambulance to the same hospital.

Some fights were a draw. Neither of us won. In one small town in Iowa, the carnival was set up around the town square. The crowds were so great we could hardly get to the ring. I was matched with a young fighter who'd been Heavyweight Boxing Champion of the Far East Command of the U.S. Air Force. He wanted to become a professional wrestler. Maybe he is now. He looked just like Elvis Presley and knew it. He hit me hard. I bloodied his nose. We went at each other for real. Time expired, and neither of us had pinned the other.

I left the ring first. The crowd was starting to leave, but they opened up to let me through. As I reached the exit, a young sorehead stepped in front of me to block my way. He was six feet tall and seething. He threw a punch at me. I saw it coming and ducked. I shoved him away and was about to land a punch of my own, when he grabbed a small baby from his wife's arms and held it up in front of his face. I couldn't wait to get to the bally. Grabbing the microphone from the talker I shouted "I want that S.O.B. who took a punch at me. No rules! No time limit! No referee! Anything goes!" I was livid with rage.

But of course the young man was nowhere to be seen. He and his wife (and baby) had sneaked out the other side of the tent.

You may think I'm exaggerating the size of the crowds at these events, but I'm not. I remember one small town in Kansas where the gate was so great and the crowds so continuous I did *eighteen fights* in one day! The population of the town couldn't have been more than 1,100, counting dogs, cats, and chickens. By daybreak, at least 6,000 people had shown up! Don't ask me where they all came from. I don't know. But there they were. Our usual hour to open the midway was noon. Here, we were forced to get it going at 6:45 in the morning! Our first At' Show—a sellout—was at 7:10 a.m.!

I worked until 2:00 in the afternoon without a break. Then I walked away. Every one of our fighters followed me. We were all so tired, hungry, and worn out we didn't care how much the boss ranted and raved. Potential ticket buyers milled around outside the tent, but with us gone he couldn't make a dime. But then, of course, neither could we. After an hour or so, I came back and so did the others. We finally closed for good at 1:10 A.M. the next morning!

That, incidentally, was the stand where the boss tried to cheat us. (We got our rightful pay, though, as I've already said).

Most At' Show owners were professional wrestlers who worked these enterprises in their off-season. They were all well-built, in perfect physical shape, and could take care of themselves in just about any situation. I remember one time in Wisconsin when our main challengers were university wrestlers. We did about average, because they were hard to beat. Tough.

As soon as one had finished his match, another would show up for the next one. Jesse was running the At' Show at that time and announced the matches would stick to Collegiate Amateur Wrestling rules. And so they did, until Friday night.

The university boys had a special wrestler they considered unbeatable. They demanded a match with Jesse himself. I tried to tell them they were making a mistake. Jesse had fought in southern states like Texas, Louisiana, Alabama, and Mississippi. When his name was on a promoter's advertising, it drew full-houses. He was top class.

The university wrestlers insisted, so into the ring went Jesse. I won't string it out. In spite of an audience cheering

100% for their champion, Jesse pinned him in just over a minute. The match was scheduled to be five.

I've never forgotten how Jesse handled the aftermath. On Saturday, the last day of the fair, Jesse himself was on the bally. The crowd was in an ugly mood. There were angry shouts at Jesse. "You beat our coach last night! We don't like it!" That kind of thing. Jesse asked if any members of the university wrestling team were in the crowd. Many were. So was their coach, the man Jesse had pinned last night. Jesse got them all to come up on the bally, introduced each by name, and complimented the coach on his work. "You've got a great bunch of wrestlers."

He went on to say "You've all upheld the spirit of Amateur Collegiate Wrestling in an outstanding way. My fighters and I want to formally recognize this. So we've gotten together to make a donation of two hundred and fifty dollars for equipment, or anything else you can use."

The crowd cheered. Once again, money talked.

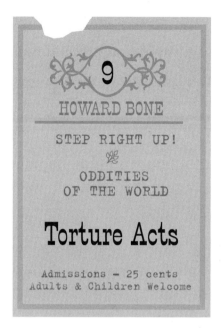

9

HOWARD BONE

STEP RIGHT UP!
❀
ODDITIES
OF THE WORLD

Torture Acts

Admissions — 25 cents
Adults & Children Welcome

From pain in At' Shows it's not a big step to pain in torture acts.

It was nothing, for instance, to become "The Human Pin Cushion" and repeatedly stick an eight-inch hat pin through my flesh and watch the blood ooze out, or, in the end, to court death itself in my scariest turn, "The Man Who Can't Be Hung."

Probably "fakir acts" would be a more accurate description of some of the side show stunts I did. "Fakir" as in Fakirs of the Middle East, India, and Africa. What Webster's Dictionary calls ". . . mendicants . . . wonder-workers . . . impostors." Impostors? Well . . . I'll say this about those acts: DON'T TRY THEM. Be warned. You can hurt yourself badly if you do. You can even kill yourself. You have to know how to do it.

Take "Walking on Broken Glass," for instance. It looks sensational. In my bare feet I step into a box of shards—step in and walk around on them! But, I warn you NOT TO TRY IT. It involves a difference between the pieces of razor-sharp broken glass you show to the spectators, and the pieces you actually walk on. But it's not as simple as that. You have to know exactly how to do it.

Then there's "Climbing a Sword Ladder." I'd make a ladder of actual fighting swords by laying them across two braces—sharp edges up! Then, again in my bare feet, I'd proceed to climb this stairway of cutlery. Lo and behold, no injury. But again I warn you: DON'T TRY IT! The danger it offers is REAL!

You have to know how to do it.

"The Iron Tongue" is another act I did for many years. I'd demonstrate the sharpness of a large butcher's hook—and in the other hand I'd hold a short thin wire cable. I'd dangle this line above a weight on the floor. Every side show had buckets for one thing or another, and sand and earth are everywhere. So I'd fill a bucket with sand for the weight. That way, I'd only have to carry the hook and line with me.

"You sir—come up please, and lift that pail. Is it heavy?"

The mark can barely lift it. (I'd try to pick the weakest-looking man in the crowd for the job.) He'd grin and nod his head or say "Yep!" or something equally expressive.

"Now, sir—will you please attach that line onto the pail of sand." He'd do so. There was a snap on the end of the line to make it easy for him. I'd then place my end of the line over the hook. It had a small closed loop on it for the purpose. Then, boldly and deliberately, I would insert the hook into my mouth so it rested on my tongue. The hook-up to the bucket of sand brings me to a leaning position. With mouth open so everybody can see the hook, and with arms extended out from my sides, I slowly straighten up. Slowly, up comes the heavy bucket of sand, apparently through tongue-power alone! It never failed to get a response.

Is it the same hook whose sharpness I've shown? Or a different one that's been switched? I'll never tell. As I said before PLEASE DON'T TRY IT! Don't try any of these. The only way to learn these things is under the careful supervision of someone who is skilled in their presentation.

I learned "The Man Who Can't Be Hung" from an old side show magician in Tacoma. The first time I tried it I nearly died. In fact, coming as close as possible to death is its whole power as an attraction.

In performance, I'd loop a one-inch rope around my neck in a simple overhand knot. I'd pick two genuine huskies out of the crowd and have them come up onstage. The rope would extend several yards from my neck on either side. If these ends were to be pulled tight, the pressure would strangle me—just as old-time hangings used to strangle the condemned. Yet that is exactly what I'd instruct these two muscular bozos from the audience to do: to pull on the ends. I'd tell them not to hold back—to pull with all their might . . . and believe me, some of those steel workers around Pittsburgh or Gary were awesome! The rope would tighten around my neck. I would become nearly unconscious. I'd fall to my knees. But at the finish I survived, and got to my feet to acknowledge the applause.

DO NOT TRY THIS.

I cannot be too emphatic.

DO NOT TRY THIS.

It is life threatening to say the least. Once more: you have to know how to do it!

I sometimes think back to myself as the trembling boy who was afraid to do a simple magic trick at a birthday party, and compare this to the roughneck I'd become. But you know something? I still got butterflies in my stomach whenever it was my turn "to dance onstage." No matter how many times I'd rolled up my sleeves and faced the crowd with cards, coins, hat pins, swords, hooks, or ropes around my neck, it was like the first time all over again. Sure, I'd gotten used to the showing off. But that's a different thing from what a person feels inside just before he has to make a bunch of strangers believe what he's doing is magical or real.

Of course, "real" depends on what you think of as "real." The fact is, every one of those acts inflicted pain on my body. That was how real they were to me. The effect on the crowd was something else. Did they believe they were really seeing an ungimmicked presentation? If they only stopped to think, they'd realize no one can do such acts day after day, week after week, year after year, unless there's some trick method of doing it. But our livelihood depended on the mark's NOT thinking.

I found early on that the more horrifying it was, the better they liked it and the more tickets we sold. Each feat was an individual act in the 10-in-one. I was paid by the act when I was in the side show. So the more acts I could do, the more money I'd make. If I was pandering to a caveman mentality . . . well, it was a mentality I didn't invent. It seems to linger on in all of us.

10

HOWARD BONE

STEP RIGHT UP!
❧
ODDITIES
OF THE WORLD

Girl Shows

Admissions — 25 cents
Adults & Children Welcome

"Velma" made their eyeballs fall right out of their heads. She was the main attraction on the free bally for our Girl Show. Every time I brought her onto the platform, a tremendous tip of farm boys formed in front of the tent to watch her pelvis do its stuff. It had a mind of its own, that pelvis. Incredible, the way she could manipulate it!

I say "farm boys," but the same glandular agitation that stirred the rustics brought city boys to the ticket box as well. These were the days of *Click* and *Pic* magazines, and even *Life* was sometimes considered racy. Girl Shows were one of the few ways a repressed male could find out about women.

Shows like "The Streets of Paris" and "Artists & Models" were a prominent part of the back end of every midway. The one I remember best, for which I was number two talker and inside lecturer, was called "The Sultan's Harem." I'd bring out Velma, dressed in a gauzy nautch-girl outfit, as low-slung as possible, flashed with bangles and bells, and she'd go into a sample of her dance. Brother! Could she ever make those baubles jingle!

She was a girl with flaming red hair, language that would put a stevedore to shame, and one of the nicest people I've ever known. When she wasn't batting her eyes at the marks, or performing her red-hot hoochie-koochie inside the tent, she was doing things like tending to some sick carny, cooking up chicken soup on the little Sterno stove she carried. I came in on her once between shows and found her holding a book in her hand. She'd been reading it. I couldn't believe my eyes: it was a Bible.

"Step right up, gents! We got 'em! We got 'em all! And here's just a sample of what's inside: (*Velma steps onto the platform*), Princess Arabia, with a taste of the hoochie-koochie she used to do for the Sultan himself before she escaped to the U.S.A. (*Velma goes into her pelvis dance. She bumps toward the crowd*). Be careful, son, she might knock you over! (*The young man nearest the bally steps back, to muted crowd laughter*). Now, you're probably wondering if she's got that red hair in . . . er . . . 'other places' on her body? Why don't you find out? All it takes is twenty-five cents, two bits, one quarter of a dollar . . . for a million dollar show! Beauties gathered from the royal harems of the world! And it's all yours! If you're old enough to see this show, you're old enough to buy a ticket! Only two bits! Come on in . . . we won't tell . . ."

Sometimes we had a shill who'd make a big deal of stepping up to the ticket box and plunking down his twenty-five cents. Mostly, though, the bolder of the crowd would start the parade and the rest of the men and youths would follow—furtively, some of them, but they'd buy. We never turned anyone away—those quarters were what we were after—and man, woman, or child, in they went.

What did they see?

For the most part, very little you'd consider salacious today. We had a total of six girls. They all did a sexy little dance, some of them quite awkwardly. As the inside lecturer as well as the talker, I introduced each in turn.

"Here's Esmerelda—direct from the harem of the Shah of Persia!"

Then "Esmerelda" would do her dance, a brief hip-shaking number. For music, we had a costumed three-piece band that played its version of oriental tunes, and some dancers had finger-cymbals.

"Esmerelda" was no more the girl's real name than was "Princess Arabia" the name of the red-haired Velma. In fact "Velma" was probably not even Velma's real name either. Most of the girls came from rural Arkansas or from the boondocks somewhere, young women escaping into the big world. They all went by their first names, which I figured were not their original ones. But what did I care? None of them had come within a stone's throw of a real harem and it was all make-believe anyway.

But not to the marks. They'd stand there ogling the girls dancing, their jaws slack, their eyes burning. Some just stared as if in a trance. Others concentrated on the girls' crotches or breasts or asses. There was mighty little to see, but their imagination gave them the thrill they were after. As for the revelation whether or not Velma's red hair was in "other places" on her body, it never came to pass. They never did get the answer I'd promised. But with all the other female allurements on hand, nobody ever complained.

The girls were really quite circumspect. It was the marks who slavered. But I shouldn't give the impression of total innocence on our part. We played as strong as we dared, stronger in some locations than others. Skimpier bras, G-strings instead of panties, and sometimes a flash of total nudity—if the girls weren't ready to do this they weren't hired. Of course, no matter where we showed, the police usually got a payoff so as not to interfere. Most of the time, the law was right there on opening day to collect or shut us down. You can be sure the side show owner had a fistful of mazuma to hand out on *that* day.

Some place in Georgia, I think it was, we got a surprise: no law. No cops, no sheriff. We were puzzled.

An old battered pickup sputtered onto the lot. The man who got out was a heavy-set rube in farmer's bib overalls, and a three-day growth of beard. I was carrying some props into the side show tent. He motioned me over to him. What's this? I thought, a plea for free passes?

"You drink booze?"

"No, sir," I said. I had my share of vices but that wasn't one of them.

"Know anybody who does?"

I knew plenty who did, but I didn't mention any names. I merely nodded my head.

"Suppose'n you go take some orders. I got the best moonshine in the county."

I didn't quite know what to make of it, but I didn't want any trouble with the locals so I did as he asked. He hadn't said anything about money, except that he didn't want any in advance. He'd be back that afternoon with the 'shine. Sounded like a trap to me. I gave him the order, but I didn't give him any names—especially not mine.

"Watch out for the sheriff," I called as he rattled off in his truck.

At about 5 o'clock that afternoon who shows up but the sheriff himself—complete with marked car, uniform, badge, holstered gun, everything. Oh-oh, I figured. We've got trouble.

I started to get the carnival boss, who could probably pay him off, when the sheriff motioned to me. Reluctantly I went over to him. Without a word he took me to the trunk of his car, opened it, and revealed two large boxes of bottled moonshine.

"I said I'd be back," he remarked.

The grubby fat man had shaved and gotten into a uniform. He and the sheriff were one and the same. The sheriff was the town bootlegger! The two of us carried the moonshine to the side show tent. The carnies who had ordered it paid him his money, and off he went. But not before he'd asked for passes to the show. "My nephew wants to see it." Sure he does, I thought. It's you and your buddies who want to come. I gave him all the passes I had—about eight—and he went away happy. We never saw him again, but I can tell you this: we had no trouble whatsoever with locals at that place. And I guess it really was his nephew who wanted to see the show, because a man showed up with the passes and about six or seven high school football-player types in tow.

After all of the girls performed, they stood in a row with long glitzy cloaks reaching down to their high-heeled shoes. "Thanks, girls!" I would say. "You've given us a wonderful look at . . . at what it must have been like in the harem." I'd lower my voice. "And now for the gents in the audience—and gents only—we have a special added attraction. Behind that curtain over there is a seventh girl I'm sure you won't want to miss. She's not from a harem, she's from Paris, France, home of the Folies Bergere. And you know what that's like. We call her Mademoiselle Eve, because she wears exactly what Eve wore for Adam . . . and I'm not talking about fig leaves. It's cost us a pretty penny to bring her to this country, so we must ask a few cents to see her: just a donation of fifteen cents and you can go back of the curtain and look to your heart's content."

This was of course our Annex for that particular Girl Show. I remember another show where we didn't have a nude girl. We had a hermaphrodite.

"Is it a man? Is it a woman? Well, gents, you can decide for yourself. Our 'maphadite' is real and alive. You'll hear him—or her—tell a fascinating life story, even as you see what she—or he—is talking about. It's completely educational . . ."

"Maphadite" was our version of "Hermaphrodite." It's what the man in the street called them. And we always stressed the "educational" nature of the turn.

The reputation of Girl Show girls was unsavory. Notice I say "reputation." Some of them hooked on the side, I suppose, but most of the come-hither eye contact with the marks was simply a way to get them to buy tickets. Some of the girls were married. Others stayed with the show only a town or two and then left. Most were young—all claiming to be 21, although I'm sure in all the different shows I was on we must have had some well-filled-out 16-year-olds . . . and probably one or two pushing fifty. The girls were strictly forbidden to go out with towners, and we carnies were warned not to touch them. But rules and regulations can be broken and frequently were. After all, these were healthy young women, in the midst of horny young men. I wish the "healthy" part was always true, but I'm afraid it wasn't. The clap was a common ailment, and always, without exception, the declaration was "I got it from a toilet seat."

How Velma came on the show gives you an idea of the kind of happenstance that brought the girls to us. The first thing I ever heard her say as she strolled up to the Girl Show manager while we were raising the tent, was:

"I thought you fuckers would never get here!"

How's that for an opening line when you're looking for a job? It seems she was making a jump with another show when her car broke down in this little Missouri town where our own carnival was to appear at the county fair. She was broke herself, so she simply decided to wait the few days it took us to get there. She'd slept in her disabled automobile, and lived off eggs stolen from a farmer's hens. She'd hardboiled them on her Sterno stove.

One girl had left us after the last town, so the owner hired her. This followed an "interview" where she showed him how she could dance.

"The broad stripped right down to nothing, just like I wasn't there!" the owner told me afterward. He never did say if anything else happened. But I don't think so. She stayed away from him and me, except in a purely social way, and seemed to have so little interest in men we began to wonder if she was a dyke or something. She was still on the show when I left to go to another one, and the last I heard, she'd married some dude in Virginia and had a couple of kids.

Girl Shows don't exist any more. At least, if they do, I don't know about them. Times have changed. You can go to almost any beach today and see more than we ever revealed in the Girl Shows.

Girl Shows, in the old-fashioned sense, probably couldn't survive today even if someone was foolish enough to try. Women see them as exploitive, and I suppose in one sense they were. But they brought to the backwaters of the nation an opportunity to step into the world of sex without danger. Farm and city males alike found in Girl Shows, as they found in the whole carnival atmosphere, a way to escape for a moment from the narrow strictures of their lives, and abandon themselves briefly to the fantasies in their minds.

A Postscript:

When I played the Georgia spot years after the moonshine incident, I asked around about the bootlegging sheriff. They told me the Feds had caught him and he had died in prison. I couldn't help but feel sad about that. He may have been leading a double life, but he was an honest man.

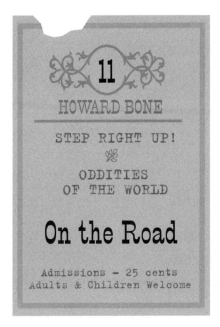

11

HOWARD BONE

STEP RIGHT UP!
❀
ODDITIES
OF THE WORLD

On the Road

Admissions — 25 cents
Adults & Children Welcome

I was driving a broken-down car on the circus route to Marathon, Florida when a storm hit. Normally, I'd pull off to the side of the road and wait it out if it was really a bad one. But I was right over the Atlantic Ocean itself, on the highway to the Keys. I couldn't see any place to pull off or even turn around and head back to the mainland. The wind blew like Billy-be-damned and rain slashed across my windshield so violently I could hardly see ten feet in front of me.

Please God, I thought, don't let me be washed into the sea. Please let this old jalopy make it! I inched along. It was the only thing to do. I didn't want to be rear-ended. As the storm roared on, the wind, the rain, the slow relentless pace of travel, put me into a kind of trance, the sort where your mind wanders. I thought of other storms . . .

Sandstorms. The wind can reach a hundred miles an hour, like it did one time in New Mexico. The cops came to the showgrounds to warn us it was on the way—which proves not every man with a badge is after you. The police radio said it would strike in about two hours.

You should have seen the action! Everyone pitched in. On the side show we took all the props off the stages and placed them on the ground. Our tent was up, of course—all 120 feet of its length, 40 feet of its width—but we lowered it and staked it securely by shortening the ropes attached to iron stakes we drove. We maneuvered the show trucks into position to block the wind. Then we high-tailed it for shelter.

A minute later the sandstorm hit. I had taken refuge in the cab of one of the trucks, with doors locked and windows tight. I never felt such wind. It rocked that heavy truck like a boat on the ocean and I was afraid the thing would tip over.

The tumult passed. Cautiously I got out and joined the others to see what damage had been done. Plenty. Even with extra cables attached, the Ferris Wheel had been tipped off its base. It must have taken fifty of us to horse it back into position. Its paint had been scoured off—just as it had been from our trucks.

Our own tent survived, thanks to our emergency measures, but the Girl Show tent . . . well, that was a different story. It had been brand-new and cost $20,000. But the operator and his girls had chosen to stay in a downtown hotel, instead of coming out and taking it down. What they saw when they got there after the sandstorm was their beautiful new tent literally cut to shreds. And no insurance, either.

Then there was that tornado in Oklahoma. We'd had tornadoes before, but I remember this one because of what happened afterward. We had done a staking job, same as for the sandstorm. Afterward, six of us—three on each side—walked slowly around our tent, inspecting it for tears and rips. Strangely, we could hear a rooster crowing. The sound was muffled and far away, yet somehow curiously close.

With a flashlight in hand, because it was dark under the canvas, I crawled beneath each section in succession to see if there'd been any damage. The crowing continued.

I pushed farther under the deflated tent. There, in the center, was a crockery jug, demijohn size. The sound seemed to be coming from there. I brought it out. One of the guys got a sledge hammer, carefully cracked it open, and out popped a rooster. Don't ask me how, but that tornado had blown a full-grown rooster into the jug!

Earthquakes were something I never got used to in California. Thunder and lightning were common in mid-west downpours. Unseasonable sleet and snow sometimes bedeviled us if we stayed too long above the Mason-Dixon line. But we were with it. We kept going.

Getting from one place to another could be a crap game. Only the big bosses had Cadillacs, Lincolns, or Packards. I generally drove a second-hand—or in many cases, third hand—motorized heap that sometimes would get me there on schedule, and sometimes wouldn't. "Previously owned" would have been a step up. Sometimes, depending on the show, I rode with someone else.

"Victor," the side show owner at this particular time, his wife "Cheryl," "Clyde" the fire-eater, and yours truly were traveling one July through Colorado. Clyde and I had a home-made trailer all to ourselves—if you don't count the pickled punks, canvas, poles, stakes, stages, and wardrobe we shared it with. If you picture an Airstream, or some kind of mobile home, think again. This trailer had been constructed of two-by-four bracings with chicken wire on the outside, so it was completely open to the breeze. It's a good thing Clyde and I liked fresh air, because that's where we rode. When it rained we'd cover ourselves with a piece of waterproof canvas and feel as snug as a lucky bug.

Vic and Cheryl rode in the luxury of their pickup truck—if you can call anything as dilapidated as that vehicle "luxury." The truck was in such bad shape even the auto mechanic on the carnival we'd just left gave up trying to repair it. We were all so broke we couldn't have afforded a down-payment on a penny box of matches.

We traveled from town to town on state and rural roads. There were no Interstate super-highways then. They were still in the future. We slept in the truck and trailer. As soon as it was daylight we'd get moving. No town cafes, no gas stations, no truck stops even, as the sun came up. Whenever we had a breakdown, which was all too often, we'd fix it the best we could and hope we'd soon hit a town with a charitable gas sta-tion grease monkey. In those days every gas station had a mechanic on hand.

One flat tire after another dogged us. We'd do our own repair. Finally we had no repair material left. BANG! went another tire. What now?

Oh-oh! Bad news. Here comes a car marked "Sheriff." Well, it turned out to be good news instead. The Deputy who was driving the car took us to a nearby cafe and actually bought breakfast for all of us. It seems his wife's cousin owned the place. Then he took us to a high-fenced auto junkyard to get some new (used) tires. Vic arranged to send ten dollars for a complete set (which he later did). The junk yard owner even loaned us his jack and a four-way lug wrench. Guess what. The yard was owned by the Deputy Sheriff's uncle.

We were only two and a half days late to the fair we were to play on that trip.

Not all bosses drove big new cars. "Johnny" had an old school bus he piloted from town to town. He'd been a railroader, and later the manager of one of Ripley's "Believe It Or Not" museums. He'd become so fascinated with the people of the museum, he'd gone out and borrowed money to operate his own side show. His whole family lived in that old bus.

With so many mouths to feed, and a slim budget to begin with, Johnny always had to think "economy." So when something went wrong with the transmission, Johnny decided to get a part and fix it himself. I knew a thing or two about machinery so I said I'd help him with it.

It was about 4:00 A.M. by the time we'd gotten the show torn down and packed out, so we couldn't start the transmission work until then.

We worked like Trojans and by 9:30 or 10:00 in the morning we were ready to put the transmission back in place. We stopped only long enough to eat the welcome refreshment Johnny's wife fixed for us. I remember it was a delicious chicken salad. We bolted the transmission back in place. Johnny turned the key in the ignition. The engine started right up. I climbed aboard. We were off to Guernsey, Wyoming, our next fair.

Or were we? Somehow or other we had put the new transmission part on wrong! The time-consuming process of removing it, putting it on right, tightening the bolts and screws, and starting her up once more, took place all over again. This time I waited until Johnny successfully shifted gears before I climbed aboard.

I complimented Johnny's wife on the great chicken salad she'd given us. "Oh," she said, red-faced. "That wasn't chicken. We had a bunch of canned rattlesnake meat. I used that."

I stopped eating chicken for about ten years.

Thumbing was one way to get around when there was no other transportation. Hitchhiking might take forever—especially during the war, when gasoline rationing was on and people didn't drive any more than they had to—but eventually it got you there.

Freight train boxcars took me to join a show more than once. I'd wait for an outgoing freight just beyond the switching yards, run alongside an empty box car, and hop aboard before the train picked up speed. You had to be careful, though. Those railroad bulls could be murder—literally. They were railroad "Security" and carried guns. One of them once actually took a potshot at me. I also carried a gun, but I didn't dare shoot back. I simply hid behind a handcar shed until another train came along. That was all the experience I'd had with trains before I got on a railroad show.

The railroad show I got on was a circus. I was on the side show attached to it. All circuses had side shows in those days. The train was composed of flat cars, sleeper cars, and a dining car. The dining car was known as the "Pie Wagon" or "Pie Car." It was more like a short order joint than one of your posh diners, and was open 24 hours a day—a great place to get together with other carnies or circus kinkers and cut up jackpots. (Have gabfests). The flat cars carried the circus' equipment—including our side show's. The sleepers . . . ah, what comfort! At least it seemed that way to me after bedding down under a truck, or sleeping cramped in an old car, or out in the open. My first morning, I couldn't believe I'd spent the night in a real bed!

One sleeper car was for the working men of the show (the "roustabouts"). The others were for performers and show personnel. You didn't automatically get to use them. You had to apply to the boss of the show, and they cost money. The weekly tab was deducted from your pay. Advance reservations were a must—even on big circuses like Ringling Bros. and Barnum & Bailey. The accommodation was not just a bunk— it was a private room. Not very big, to be sure. As the saying went, "You have to go to the Pie Car to change your mind!"

Sleeper cars had civilized restrooms. Two of them had showers. There were porters, and a Train Boss. The Train Boss was king of the whole shebang. His word was law. If he told you to clean up your sleeper, you did—right then. If you were having a party and he told you to pipe down, you did. If a fight started—booze was available in the Pie Car—he broke it up. Sometimes he'd send the culprit to another part of the train and the offender could return only with the Train Boss's permission. If he continued to cause trouble, he might end up sleeping on a flat car. I never did, but I knew some who did. You had an option to this punishment. Actually you had three options: 1) you could change your attitude, 2) live on a "flat," or 3) leave the show the next time the train stopped.

"Red Lighting" was the ultimate punishment. It was reserved for extreme cases, after everything else had been tried, and seemed to arise mostly in the gazonie car. In show lingo a "gazonie" is the lowest form of human life, the very bottom of the barrel. "Gazonie" was the unflattering name given to circus laborers. Many of them were O.K., but a large number were winos, potheads, escaped jailbirds, sadists, and roughnecks of the most primitive sort. They traveled in the gazonie car—a sleeper avoided by other show people if at all possible. Anything could happen in the gazonie car—and did.

One gazonie in particular had caused all sorts of trouble. He terrorized everybody in the car. He beat up a few drunks. He swaggered about like he owned the train. He never washed himself or changed his clothes. His talk was filthy and his manner was nasty. The Train Boss warned him several times, telling him if he didn't straighten up, he'd be Red Lighted. The third warning brought a string of curses and a rejoinder that the Train Boss could kiss him "where the sun don't shine!"

The Train Boss got six of us together, collared the gazonie, escorted him struggling and cursing to the vestibule at the end of the car, and as we approached the yards, threw him off the moving train. That was Red Lighting.

Yes, it was a brutal punishment, but please remember, this was a brutal man. In the show world you're given a chance, and if you don't take it, no quarter is given. It's a rough life, no question.

The man we had thrown off the train showed up bloody and bruised the next day. He came to the midway with several police officers to press charges.

"I don't know what you're talking about," the owner said, innocent as a newborn babe. "He must have been drunk and fell off accidentally." The cops turned and left, with the snarling gazonie stomping after them. That was the last we saw of him. When you're with it, you play by the rules.

Those railroad sleeping cars were a far cry from automobile breakdowns, hitchhiking, and boxcars to get where you were going. You never had to worry about bad roads. And you certainly never had to battle your way through a storm . . .

A storm. My mind came back to the present. Marathon, out in the Florida Keys, could not be too far away now. The wind still blew with fierceness and the rain continued to lash my car as I crept along the highway that bridged the ocean. But up ahead, I could see taillights. They were on a truck. It was one of ours—a circus truck loaded with ring curbs and equipment. Then, in my rearview mirror, I could make out the headlights of another truck bearing down on me from behind. It's not moving very fast, I thought, so I'm in no danger. It, too, turned out to be one of ours.

Between these two trucks, like a precious treasure protected front and rear, I finally pulled into the showgrounds at Marathon, where the storm passed through, and the sun smiled again.

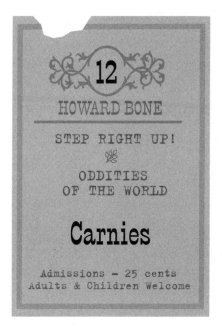

12

HOWARD BONE

STEP RIGHT UP!

ODDITIES
OF THE WORLD

Carnies

Admissions — 25 cents
Adults & Children Welcome

"**B**y the twenty-four swinging balls of the twelve apostles!" is the most colorful expression I ever heard uttered during my years on the road. It was spoken in a state of complete exasperation by a concessionaire whose stand—and life savings—had been destroyed in a blow-down.

Not every carny used blasphemy or profanity. Roxie "Scissor Bill" Moore didn't. Roxie was the main ticket seller, boss canvasman, electrician, and second in command of one side show I was on. He was around sixty when I knew him and he never cussed. It was always "I'll be a dirty scissor bill!"

"Shifty" Watkins seldom cussed except when he was at the wheel of a carnival truck. I rode shotgun with him one time during a jump through, I think, Alabama. By "shotgun" I don't mean firearms—I mean the guy next to the driver who watches for route arrows put up by the 24-hour man, pointing the way to the next stand. As we rolled through various towns we saw police officers directing traffic at main intersections. In those days that was a common sight. If we had to stop for the light, Shifty would always smile brightly and wave at the cop. At the same time, under his breath he'd mouth "you goddam stupid asshole." The officer couldn't hear him. At least Shifty *thought* the cop couldn't hear him. But at one stoplight the law of averages caught up with him. The cop grimly motioned us over and asked to see Shifty's driver's license. Shifty had not one, but *eight* of them—all in different names—and a string of violations a mile long. Shifty ended up in the pokey, and I was stranded. I couldn't drive at that time.

Luckily, another show truck came through town. The cop stopped it. The "shotgun" took over Shifty's truck, and we went on our way. Shifty? I don't know what happened. I expect he got the book thrown at him, but who knows? I never saw him again.

It turned out the policeman was hard of hearing and had become an expert lip-reader! He'd known what Shifty said, even though he couldn't hear him.

There were many carnies who never blued the air at all, and I was one of them. Well . . . hardly ever. It wasn't that I was so goody-goody, it was my upbringing. I'd had my mouth washed out with Fels Naptha soap a few times when I was a kid, and if you've ever been through that experience you know it tends to moderate your speech.

One of the non-cussers was a boy who came on the show at age 17. We called him "Gopher" because we sent him everywhere to "go-fer" everything. We tipped him for his pains, but being so young he was still low man on the totem pole. "Wilma Mae," the show's owner, made him bring his mother to the lot and had her sign a paper before hiring him. No sense in being hassled for using underage help. Gopher sold tickets on the front of the show.

Gopher was a nice kid. I liked him. Somewhere along the line someone gave him a puppy. It was the love of his life. He kept it loosely tied next to the ticket box while he was working, and when he wasn't working he exercised it, watered, fed, and cleaned up after it.

On the show, too, was "Chief Raincloud," who was our Fire Eater at the time. Chief Raincloud appeared in the most spectacular American Indian wardrobe I've ever seen. It included a full-fledged, gloriously authentic-looking Sioux war bonnet. Gopher thought he was a real Indian, because he was dark skinned, dark eyed, and black haired. Actually, he was of Italian descent. But he'd lead Gopher on about Indian tribes, customs, and history, letting drop the fact that many Indians considered cooked dog a great delicacy. He'd eye the puppy and smack his lips when he said this.

Gopher thought he meant it, and every time Chief Raincloud came around, Gopher would make sure the fast-growing dog was well out of the way. But the Chief wouldn't let up. The climax came one day when he told Gopher he had gathered a bunch of vegetables and wanted to buy the dog in order to make stew. He was only kidding, of course, but Gopher picked up a stick and rushed the Chief. He chased him right off the lot. I had to tell Gopher the truth: that the Chief was only joking. They became good friends sometime later.

The last I knew, Chief Raincloud was teaching Gopher how to be a fire eater.

I ran into "Hobo Pete" on a three-ring circus. He was the boss canvasman—one of the best in history. He had to supervise the raising of the big top and all the other tops on the show. He had to make sure they went up the right way in the right place at the right time—and they always did. The canvas truck, the stake truck, and the tent crew were all his responsibility. The side show tent always got put up before the crew had quite finished the big top, so side show equipment could be moved in, and the show opened for business (and for making money) right away. Moving equipment into a tent takes a "pointer." He's the man who "points" to what goes inside the tent. The work crew—the gazonies—usually has greenhorns on it, and somebody has to tell them what to do. Hobo Pete picked me as his side show Pointer.

You towners—when you get to the lot, all you know is that the tents are up. You never give it a second thought. But getting the job done is a harrowing operation. Wet canvas from rain at the last town, all manner of terrain to contend with—earth, mud, asphalt, inexperienced crewmen—it's all very stressful for the man in charge, to say the least. But drunk or sober, Hobo Pete got the big top and all the other tops up and down right on schedule.

He'd gotten his name from years before, when he lived in hobo camps, and "drunk," I'm afraid, describes his condition much of the time. When the circus season ended, he'd go on one long binge. But when the season started again, owners knew Pete would be back. He'd keep his word and be there—unless he was in jail, which was not infrequently. Some owners were known to bail him out, just so they could have the advantage of the best in the business on their show.

Of course, Hobo Pete didn't need an off-season layoff to hit the bottle. We were going to be in one town for two or three days, so after the tops were all up, Pete got the O.K. to leave the lot. He planned to get a motel room for the night, wash up in a real bathroom, sleep in a full-sized bed, and no doubt partake of the sauce in comfort. After our shows were over for the evening, I went into town with a couple of side show cronies, and what do you know?—here was Pete at one of the local night clubs. He was on the way to getting loaded, smashed, blotto. Payday had just taken place and he flashed a large roll of bills. As we started to leave, we noticed two suspicious looking characters getting friendly with Pete. So we turned around and, over his protests, eased him out of there, took him to his motel room, and put him to bed. He was belligerent as a doped up bull.

"Hey Pete, you lousy drunk, turn over!" We could only get his shoes and sox off—nothing else. But In the process we saw how much cash he had been carrying—hundreds of dollars! We couldn't allow him to go out again carrying that much money. He'd be rolled for sure. We managed to shift him enough to take the bankroll from his pocket, left him a few dollars for pocket money, and went on our way.

About noon the next day, word got around the circus that Pete hadn't shown up. This wasn't like him, even when he'd been drinking. By two in the afternoon he still wasn't there. Some of the kinkers wanted to call and see if he was in jail. Others said we should check the hospital. We went to the motel room he'd rented. Nothing.

At 2:30 P.M. the door of one of the parked show trucks flew open, and out roared Pete. He had left the motel last night and slept off his stupor in the cab of the vehicle. He'd been right under our noses. "Where's the son-of-a-bitch who robbed me?" he bellowed. "I'll shoot the thieving bastard!" We quickly produced his money—with trembling hands, I might add, because Pete meant what he said when he was sober. We tried to explain we had taken it for his own good. I think he knew we spoke the truth. But all he said, in no uncertain terms, was "Leave me alone, you bunch of freaks!"

"Slim" Kuchinski was the side show's "Human Skeleton." He was over six feet tall and weighed only slightly more than a hundred pounds. The "Fat Man" on our show was called . . . need I tell you? . . . "Tiny." He was pictured on the bannerline as "Baby Bobby" and the garish painting exaggerated his weight by more than a hundred pounds. He actually tipped the scales at around 370, but the banner said 519.

Slim and Tiny were in their fifties. They went everywhere together. Working side by side in the 10-in-1 to emphasize their contrast, I guess they simply continued the togetherness offstage. Or maybe it was merely that they both liked their liquor. Somewhere in their travels they'd purchased a three-year-old Cadillac. In a South Carolina town where we played for several days they took it into a garage for repair. Slim, who always drove, slipped over to a nearby joint for a Cafe Royal, then returned to watch the repair of the Caddy on the hoist. Suddenly the car's back side door opened and Tiny stepped out. He planted his feet in thin air and plummeted to the floor with a crash. He'd been sleeping in the back seat. The only reason he wasn't hurt was because he was drunk.

On the following Friday morning, Slim was involved in an incident. About 10:00 A.M., feeling an urgent call of nature and not wanting to go all the way to the midway donniker, Slim slipped into the woods backing the show lot.

No sooner had he gotten in than he came streaking out. "Help! Help! Oh God, help!" he screamed.

I had my gun in hand and the hammer cocked as I ran to see what was the matter. Other carnies, hearing him, did the same. Nearly everybody carried a gun.

"There's a dead man back there!" Slim cried. "Call the police! Oh, help! Help!"

I calmed the over-wrought Slim and joined the others in the woods. Sure enough, a dead body lay among the trees. Someone did call the police. The coroner came and took the corpse away. He figured it was a tramp who'd built a fire in the woods and then, intoxicated beyond sensibility, had fallen over into the blaze and died of smoke inhalation.

Slim and Tiny stayed sober for a long time after that—a week or two, at least.

Once on a truck circus, I had a propman friend, "Drinks" Carter. In addition to his prop work, Drinks drove the water wagon for extra money. Each morning, he'd fill the big tank, using a fire hose, then make the rounds delivering water to circus animal trainers, the cookhouse, and each of the trailers where the big top performers lived. He made still more dough by selling soft drinks to the circus hands. He'd buy various soda-pops, put them in a tub filled with ice, and sell them to thirsty canvasmen, prop men, elephant handlers, side show crew, and anyone who wanted them.

There was only one problem. With his water wagon and prop chores taking so much of his time Drinks couldn't always watch over the tub of soft drinks—and someone was stealing from him. He watched whenever he could, trying to catch the culprit, but no luck. He asked me what he should do.

I thought it over. "Buy several bottles of croton oil," I told him. "Mix it with some lemon-lime soda, and mark the bottles so you'll know which ones contain it. Then see who gets a bad case of the shits."

Sure enough, the next morning about 2:00 A.M. Drinks was awakened by moaning and groaning outside the water truck cab where he was sleeping. In the shadows he saw a man crouched in a squatting position, with his pants down. A half-empty soda bottle lay nearby. Drinks gave him time enough to pull up his trousers. Then he seized him by the collar and dragged him kicking and yelling to the Boss Canvasman's trailer. In short order the offender found out about circus and carnival justice for thieves. In the middle of the night he was manhandled to the edge of the lot and told to "hit the highway and don't come back."

Crude. Rough. Primitive. Yes. But on the road it's survival of the fittest. Those who steal get short shrift.

Booze played a part in all too many dismal episodes. A carnival seems to be one place where an alky can drink to his heart's content and yet keep his job—as long as he's sober enough to do it. The man who was once the ticket seller on our show had blood that was ninety-nine percent Jack Daniels. He went to town one time, feeling no pain. In the five-and-dime store he pawed through the shaving lotion containers. Picking up a bottle of Bay Rum After Shave Lotion he bawled at the top of his lungs: "Where the hell's the bartender?" He put up such a fuss when they tried to get him out of the store, he was arrested for public intoxication and spent three days in jail. He was lucky to have a job when he got back out. The show's owner knew he did a good job and decided it would be more work to replace him than to take him back.

"Red" was the nickname of a carny with . . . what else? . . . red hair. He was a side show magician like me. I've forgotten why we were together, but we were. One of us was probably "at liberty" and visiting the one who was working. Anyway, we went to a restaurant to eat.

We got a friendly hello from the cashier, and returned a cordial greeting. In the process we stole several blank meal checks sitting by the cash register. During the meal Red had to go to the restroom. While he was away, I made my cream container disappear before the astonished eyes of the waitress and the other customers. When Red came back, I accused him of stealing it. Quick to pick up the gag, he made several passes at the waitress' head, and produced it seemingly from her hair. After the meal we pretended our checks were totaled wrong. We argued with the waitress. She got the manager. Our voices rose to a loud indignant level. Red blatted out that the food was poisoned and we'd been cheated on cost. In full view of the customers we angrily tore up our checks in little pieces.

It was all too much, of course. We weren't on the midway now. And we couldn't plead drunkenness. We were stone cold sober. By the time we magically produced the original checks, the waitress was in tears, and the owner was threatening to call the police. We had staged our little joke in bad taste, no question. Our apologies and extra-large tip did no good. The owner kicked us out of the restaurant and told us never to come back again.

So boozers weren't the only ones who could get into trouble.

I never looked for anyone to help me when the chips were down. In carnival life you're on your own. That's why I was surprised one time in Idaho, when I was still on Athletic Shows. I'd been catapulted out of the ring, and lay there on the floor at the feet of the spectators, seemingly unconscious. My eyes were closed and the count was going "nine, ten, eleven . . ." Suddenly I felt hands under me, and a voice whispering "Let me help you. I'm a professional boxer. I know the score." I opened my eyes and looked up at the man we later called "Champ." Champ helped me to my feet, and acting groggy and dazed, I clambered back into the ring just ahead of "twenty," (which would have counted me out) for maximum suspense. I had been playing "the bad guy" and now I was supposed to attempt my revenge. It had all been arranged beforehand. At four minutes and twenty seconds I was pinned to the mat. I lost.

As I got out of the ring, there was Champ. He stuck with me all the way to the outside bally where I talked up the next fight. He repeated his claim that he was a "professional boxer." If so, I thought, he might be a good candidate for the At' Show. His eyes lit up when I suggested it to him. He said he was interested—yes, definitely interested. After we closed for the night, I took him to see the boss. It turned out he was telling the truth. He had actually been a professional. He had the clippings to prove it: twenty-seven pro fights, sixteen knockouts. He'd fought in Madison Square Garden with a World Champion. He was indeed a "Champ." The big question was: why? Why, with such a great background, did he want to get on a lousy carnival Athletic Show? He'd be taking on all comers. There was no insurance coverage if he went to the hospital. The pay was nothing compared to what he must have been used to. Why?

With a shamed face he made a confession. He had a serious problem, he said. He'd drunk up all his winnings, was a total lush, and had turned into a bum. He needed a job badly.

The boss hired him on. We taught him what to do, which was quite different from what he had known. He became an excellent muscle-head. In many ways, Champ was childlike. We soon learned never to let him sit in the back seat when we drove from town to town. He'd put his hands over the driver's eyes and ask "Can you see? Can you see?" It was his way of letting you know he liked you—but we had enough hazards in the ring without getting them in the car.

We tried to help him kick his alcohol habit. It looked like we were winning. "Hey Professor," he'd say to me after a match, "I need a gallon of coffee right now. What I really need is a drink—but I promised . . ."

Finally, he made a decision. "I'm checking myself into the V.A. hospital for The Cure. I'm going to beat this thing forever!"

We wrote to him, all of us. We'd telephone him from town to town. He wrote back, or made collect calls to us. We wanted him to know we were rooting for him. We'd taken a shine to the guy and found an unaccustomed satisfaction in helping somebody else.

Then the letters from him grew fewer and fewer. So did the phone calls. Then we didn't hear from him at all. We were worried—all of us, including the boss. The boss had a commercial stake in the guy, true—but he also had developed a personal concern for him. Finally, the boss telephoned the Veterans Administration hospital. When he hung up he called us all into the ring. There were tears in his eyes.

"The V.A. doctor told me Champ took a weekend pass and got drunk. He managed somehow to get hold of a gun and committed suicide."

There were no fights that night.

I've often thought of Champ. He had everything to live for. He was a great friend and a great muscle-head. Maybe we did wrong, trying to change him. Maybe the carny way was the best way after all. You take a person as you find him.

STEP RIGHT UP!

ODDITIES
OF THE WORLD

Hey Rube!

Admissions – 25 cents
Adults & Children Welcome

By now I had been 15 years on the road. I'd known variety if nothing else. Side shows on carnivals and circuses. Athletic Shows. Traveling miles by thumb, rail, car, or truck. I had finally learned to drive the big rigs that hauled the shows from town to town. I had also become notorious among my coworkers. They called me "Crazy Cobra."

There's a common saying: "I'm going to run away from home and join the circus."

I expressed it somewhat differently: "I'm going to run away from the circus and join a home—a mental home."

I had gotten perilously close. I was "that crazy carny who'll try anything." Blood and guts—mine or someone else's—were nothing new to me. Fear as such didn't exist. I was hotheaded, outspoken, devious, quick with my fists, and lethal when I brought my martial arts into play.

To tell the truth, in the kind of life I was leading that sort of thing wasn't all bad. The side show drew audiences consisting of dangerous cuckoos as well as ordinary people. Perhaps the worst were the gangs.

A girl gang in New England tried to make trouble. They were tough looking broads with leather jackets, leather trousers, death's-head ornaments, colored hair, and weird face makeup applied too thick. They backed down in a hurry, though, when we said we'd call "Sergeant Kelley." Sergeant Kelley had tipped us off about gangs in the area, and said if any of them tried to give us a hard time, just use his name. Apparently he'd struck terror into their hearts. He was on the cops' gang detail and no one wanted to be nabbed by him. It would mean a trip "downtown"—not a very pleasant experience, we gathered.

Everybody wants to know about "Hey Rube!" Well, "Hey Rube" hasn't been used in 50 years. Once upon a time it was the circus cry for everyone to come running—preferably with tent stakes in hand. But the marks soon got to know what it meant. When I was on the shows it was "Signal 25"—not shouted by some hapless showhand being attacked, but broadcast over the loudspeakers that replaced vocal projection and megaphones on showgrounds.

I was in a few "Signal 25's" during my career. They were usually caused by some belligerent liquored-up towner trying to take on the world—starting with us. Most of the time, if the carny was me, I could manage it alone, but sometimes it got out of hand, at which time "Signal 25" brought more bruisers down on the troublemaker than he'd ever seen in his life.

Play fair? I never played fair. The object was to stay alive, not play fair. It was no game.

One hot humid night on a carnival in New Jersey several members of a gang tried to crash the side show through the open back sidewall. We had rolled it up to let air circulate. The hot lights were brutal on us, and we were all sweating like pigs. I blocked their way.

"The ticket box is out front, gentlemen. If you want to come in, buy a ticket like everybody else. Otherwise, stay the hell out!" I sounded tough, and meant to.

They tried three times. Each time I told them to get lost. The fourth time it didn't work. They'd gathered their buddies—a dozen or more—and rushed us en masse. Waving chains, iron bars, and knives, they yelled and cursed at the spectators. They pushed them roughly aside as they shouldered toward the stage, aiming to get at me.

I was doing a rope escape at the time and had been trussed up so I couldn't move. Or so they thought. One grinning thug with tattoos on his arms yanked me off the platform. As I fell, I escaped my bonds—the fastest magic escape on record, I think—and was free when I hit the ground. My attacker couldn't believe his eyes. I can still see the shocked look that replaced the grin on his face.

Should I punch him? What?

Instead, I pulled one of my patented dirty tricks. I told him my right arm had broken in the fall and pleaded with him to help me straighten it out. That gave me time to reach for the Klein pliers in my rear pocket. With a vicious motion, I slashed him across the face. I'd opened the Kleins so the sharp edges were out. (I told you I'd reveal another use for them besides foiling gate crashers and untying knots!)

Blood spurted from his cheek. He sat there in a daze. I yanked him to his feet and forced him back up onto the platform. The rest of the gang was fighting show people inside the tent.

Outside, the ticket seller, alerted by one of the illusion girls, breathlessly announced "Signal 25 at the side show . . . Signal 25 at the side show . . ."

Other carnies poured in. I shouted over the battling crowd: "Hey, stop! The police are on their way." I thrust my bleeding captive forward. "If you bums don't quit, I'll *really* hurt your friend! Look at him!" My pliers were ready to clamp his ear.

He whimpered in pain. His face ran with blood. My words got across loud and clear. Outside, police sirens were whining to a stop. I pitched my bleeding prisoner down among his friends, and they fled out the back sidewall opening. The carnies who'd responded to "Signal 25" disappeared in another direction.

We had no more trouble that night, but the side show owner was not one to take chances. I'd aroused the fury of a tough bunch and they might be back. He gave me money for traveling and said I should meet the show in western Pennsylvania three days later.

Never mess with a carny—most of all one who's called "Crazy Cobra."

STEP RIGHT UP!
❦
ODDITIES
OF THE WORLD

"Crazy Cobra"

Admissions — 25 cents
Adults & Children Welcome

How did I get the name of "Crazy Cobra?"

"Crazy" you know. "Cobra" you don't. If it reminds you of snakes, you've got it.

Like I said, I'd become notorious among the carnies for doing almost anything—and they weren't far wrong. "Wild Bill" Gunderson ran the Snake Show on one long-ago carnival and when he had a particularly dangerous job of snake-handling, he'd ask me to help him because he knew I'd always say "yes." Most other carnies would give the snake show a definite miss. But not me. I just didn't give a rat's ass about anything in those days.

Wild Bill's snake show was built on the framework of a semi-trailer. Once the spectators had paid their money they could walk around a platform and look into glass cages of individual snakes. There were twelve cages in all. They contained reptiles you don't want to fool with—like Diamondback Rattlers, Boa Constrictors, poisonous snakes from Mexico, and a gigantic venomous Egyptian Cobra. There were King Snakes and others, but the cobra was the big attraction. It measured about five feet long and weighed close to twelve pounds.

Like all snakes, the cobra shed its skin, but for some reason hadn't shed over its eyes. The only way to keep it from going blind from infection was to slip the old skin off the eyes.

"You hold it down," Wild Bill said, "and I'll use these tweezers to pull off the skin."

What could be easier?

What indeed?

I tried to hold it down with a length of broom handle. It flared its hood and struck. The only reason I didn't get zapped was because I yanked back, and Wild Bill slammed down the lid of the cage just in time.

I was damned if I was going to let a mere snake beat me.

"This gimmick is no good," I said, tossing aside the piece of broom handle. "After the snake's settled down, you lift the lid. I'll reach in with my hands, grab it, and hold it up so you can get at its eyes."

Wild Bill gave me a look, said "Wait a minute," and left. He came back with an official looking paper in his hand.

"Read this," he said.

"What is it?"

"A release form in case you get bitten."

"I'm not going to get bitten—"

"Read it anyway."

I read it. It was exactly what he said it was: a form releasing Wild Bill from any responsibility, should the snake get me. I signed it where he pointed out. He also insisted I wear a long-sleeved shirt, a buttoned-up jacket, and a pair of heavy leather gloves. What the hell was he afraid of?

Slowly, so as not to disturb the cobra, he raised the top of the cage. Slowly my hand went in. With a sudden move I grabbed the cobra's head and brought it up. The big snake twitched, twisted, and flung itself about. Shit! This baby was all muscle! It tried to flare its hood but couldn't. I had an iron grip on the thing with both hands now and wasn't about to let go. Wild Bill did his trick with the tweezers and the eyes came clear. At the count of "three" I let go and he slammed the lid.

That killing machine struck once, twice, three times—all at the lid. It was mad! We were out of danger, but when Wild Bill snapped the padlock on the cage, we didn't run down the steps from the platform—we jumped!

Monkeys were another story altogether. Funny little critters. On one side show, the owner's wife, "Wendy," used to hand feed the mischievous simians herself. There were fifteen of them—all Spider Monkeys—so it was a long job. But she seemed to like it. She'd unsnap the little chain that held each one by the collar and give them their food. Then she'd re-attach the chain, which ran to a stake.

One day I was in the side show. I'd just finished my acts and was introducing the next performer when Wendy came running in. Half the monkeys had escaped! Somehow they had gotten loose and were skylarking around back of the animal show tent.

I grabbed the rope I used in one of my acts, made it into a lasso, and ran to the animal tent. Sure enough, there were the monkeys back of it, chattering and cavorting free as birds. We tip-toed softly to approach them. No good. The minute we got within ten feet they screeched and ran away from us. Various carnies kept this up until nighttime. Somebody said go get some bananas to lure them back. It didn't work.

The concessions and rides closed up. Finally, at 2:00 A.M. we threw in the towel. The monkeys could roam forever for all I cared.

But what do you know?—by morning they had all come back to the pack. I guess the little buggers got lonesome for their own kind.

I don't know which is worse, elephants or lions. I faced up to one of each at different times. Today I wonder how I had the guts. Back then, it didn't seem like a matter of guts. I was just "that crazy cobra," and took off after the escaped beasts when everybody else had the good sense to hang back.

The circus I was on presented the cat act first on the program. Most circuses do. That's because the steel-barred enclosure in the center ring—"the big cage"—can be erected before the show starts. It's made of sections. After the act is over, these sections are quickly taken down while the spotlights move to aerialists performing up above.

I was on the circus side show, of course, but I'd taken to helping "Bart," the lion trainer. For once I didn't do it because of extra pay. I did it because I'd become friends with Bart and his family. As soon as the side show shut down for the big top performance, I'd shuck my tux, jump into prop-man coveralls, and make a bee-line for the sound of the circus band. My job was simple: open and close the entrance/exit door of the big cage for Bart.

He'd been having problems with one of the new cats. This lion, a male named Gaza, was a spectacular animal. He was full-grown, beautifully maned, weighed something like 250 pounds, and when he stood on his hind legs was over six feet tall. But he hadn't quite gotten used to being in the cage, disliked the band music, and hated Bart and the straw house we had that day. By "straw house" I mean a sellout. If we'd been an old-time circus we would have put down straw for the overflow to sit on. Theatre jargon is "S.R.O.—Standing Room Only." In the circus we say "straw house."

It was a hot, uncomfortable, muggy day. Sitting on his perch in the big cage, Gaza roared repeatedly. He also started swatting the end of the rope that hung down from the net over the top of the enclosure.

Bart saw what he was doing and cracked his whip in Gaza's direction. Instead of letting loose of the rope, Gaza gave it a yank. The knot that helped hold the overhead net in place came undone. With one tremendous leap, Gaza hurtled through the opening and landed outside the cage. You never saw such pandemonium. The Equestrian Director ("Ringmaster") shouted into the microphone for everyone to keep calm. But he might as well have been whispering into the wind. The audience screamed. Prop men, candy butchers, clowns, even performers waiting at the back door in their sparkly wardrobe scattered like leaves in a gale. Audience members started a minor riot trying to get out. The band swung into "Stars and Stripes Forever," the circus emergency signal.

I picked up a piece of 2 x 4 lumber—I can't even tell you where I got it—and made for the lion. I gave him a terrific blow on the head. Instead of being cowed, Gaza charged me. I took off running up the hippodrome track like a championship sprinter. The beast was right behind me. I could feel his breath on my legs. I knew if he caught me I was a dead man. It's amazing what you can do when you have to. I whirled around, gave an unearthly yell, and stopped Gaza in his tracks. But only for a second. Just as he recovered and was about to pounce on me, four prop men darted out from behind the bandstand and threw a net over him.

You can believe that episode didn't do anything to detract from my "crazy cobra" image.

Animated movie cartoons have done a grave disservice to the animal world—and therefore to the public at large. They tend to portray elephants, for example, as big cuddly lummoxes without a mean bone in their bodies. "Mean" they may not be—I never knew a truly "mean" animal in my life. "Wild," yes, but not "mean." That characteristic is reserved for human beings. But they are definitely not cuddly creatures. Elephants can behave with total docility for months and years, and then, all of a sudden, they'll cut loose. Their trunks can reach out and toss you fifty feet. They can crush you with their sheer bulk. They can grind you into the ground with their head or rump. I'm amazed how many people used to come up to elephants in the menagerie and pet, yell, and flaunt themselves around the creatures, little knowing what danger they were in. Or could be.

Most animals, when they get loose, seem to be going on a rampage when actually they are simply confused or scared.

They are not used to the freedom and don't know where to go or what to do. I remember reading of an escaped elephant who was gunned down in the Rockies by "amateur sportsmen" (as the newspaper had it). They emptied 165 shots into the poor creature before they killed it. The owner's comment was that "the elephant had been in a truck that turned over twice, and had been in a bad mental state ever since." My God!—I'd have been in a bad mental state too.

As it was, my mental state when Belloch got loose was idiotic enough. Belloch was a young but huge female African elephant who was fairly new to circus life. "Bernie," who worked the act, set a rehearsal between shows. Luckily, no one much was around. As Belloch stood flapping her ears and waiting for her cue at the back door, she shifted her weight uneasily. She didn't want to move when her handler urged her forward. Instead, she trumpeted loudly. Finally she moved, all two tons of her. Just as she reached the center ring where she was to join the other bulls, a bandsman clashed his cymbals. This was simply part of the new music for the act, but Belloch didn't know it.

She screams in terror and breaks away from her handler. He's frozen for a few seconds as she turns and runs, trumpeting over and over again. I grab the bull hook from the handler and take off down the hippodrome track after Belloch. She vanishes out the back door and heads for the area where the big top performers have their house trailers parked. I'm right behind her. Other handlers join the chase. She bounces off several of the trailers, their occupants raging out angry and protesting, but going slack-jawed and speechless when they see what's happening.

"Stop, Belloch! Stop!" I shout.

She's headed for the showgrounds fence. Beyond are the houses, gardens, and streets of the towners. Somehow or other I manage to get alongside the speeding pachyderm—and believe me, they can hustle when they want to—and I reach her with the bull hook. It slips off. I hook her again. And again. "Stop, Belloch! Stop!"

I slowed her just enough for Bernie to get to her. He stopped her and calmed her down. She was inches short of the fence.

Did I get complimented for my efforts? Of course not. The side show owner bawled me out good and proper for risking my neck. After all, he needed me on the show.

I told him to take his job and shove it, and left in a huff. Well . . . no, I didn't. I would have under other circumstances. But circumstances have a way of changing. This "crazy carny," was about to change too. I had fallen for a girl on the circus.

Love had reared its head.

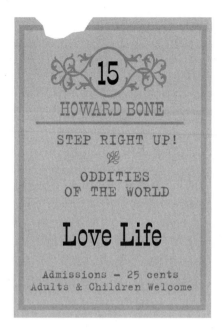

15

HOWARD BONE

STEP RIGHT UP!

ODDITIES
OF THE WORLD

Love Life

Admissions – 25 cents
Adults & Children Welcome

P ossum Belly Queens are town girls who think they've fallen in love with a carny, and act accordingly. The name comes from the "possum belly" of certain carnival semis, where there's a compartment added underneath the truck to hold tent stakes or other equipment.

Once the show is up, the compartment makes dandy sleeping quarters—dandy, that is, if you don't mind bedding down on a solid steel mattress, often without blankets or a sleeping bag. Many's the time I've slept there when nothing else was available. It's cramped and small, but at least you're off the ground and out of the rain.

You're also pretty much out of sight—which makes it a great hideaway for showhands who've got a girl in tow. Nobody really cares about such behavior, of course—except sometimes the parents of the girl. These possum belly amours generally last about the length of time the show is in town. Sometimes, though, the girl will actually leave town with the carnival.

"Eddie," a side show canvasman, had "Betsy" so stuck on him she did exactly that. She stayed with the show long enough to turn into a carny herself. Became part of the side show crew. Trouble was, Betsy was underage—15 or 16 maybe, although she certainly looked older. When her parents sicced the law on us, a Deputy Sheriff showed up to take her home. She was nowhere to be seen, so he demanded to search the side show tent. Eddie told him "go right ahead—if you've got a search warrant." The Deputy had no such document, so he gnashed his teeth and went away empty-handed. But it was a close call. Betsy had been hiding not four feet away, underneath the main stage. Finally, after six or eight weeks, the romance cooled. She phoned her parents to send her bus fare back home, which was some six hundred miles and three states away.

"Ann," the girl I'd fallen in love with, was NOT a Possum Belly Queen. She was one of the bally girls on the circus. In a nightclub they'd be called "chorus girls." In a circus they perform the same highly decorative function, only differently. They add glamour to the spec as they ride on floats or sit atop heads of the elephants. In the show they are Babylonian slaves one minute, sumptuously costumed princesses another, or, the next thing you know, flash dancers covered in sequins. Sometimes, in the "aerial ballet," they'll wear wings as they gyrate in glittering briefs and bras on their Spanish webs (cloth-covered ropes) high above the rings. Sometimes they're all aglow in black light. Ann was a definite looker, and I was attracted to her from the first. We decided to get married.

At least we decided to consider ourselves married, even though no clergyman, justice of the peace, or legal papers were involved. Ann left the circus after I had joined a carnival not far away. There, we had that old traditional carny rite known as a "Billboard Wedding."

That means we sent a notice to *The Billboard* magazine that Ann and I were going to live together as man and wife. That was the first requirement. *The Billboard* was read by everybody in outdoor show business so it was the best way to reach as many old friends as possible, and invite them to the "wedding." (*The Billboard* used to be known as the "bible of outdoor shows.")

The day of the ceremony was really the *night* of the ceremony. It took place after the rides, concessions, and side show had all closed up. Only carnival people were on the lot. The show's electrician started up the Merry-Go-Round, all lights, mirrors, and jingling oom-pah-pah. Ann and I were permitted to board only after it started moving—a neat trick if you've had a few drinks, which I had done in honor of the occasion. Normally, I don't drink—and that made it even worse.

Our wedding march was the lilting mechanical waltz from the Merry-Go-Round. Our "aisle" was the circling pathway through the rising/falling horses to the chariot seats toward which we stumbled, laughing all the way. The others woozily stationed themselves around us—the Bridesmaid, Best Man, a Flower Girl, and a Ring Bearer who was the show mechanic, bearing a faucet washer from his kit. Then "Ross," the show's owner flopped onto the seat opposite us. He had a drink in one hand and a copy of *The Billboard* in the other. Everybody was swaying and holding onto something to stay upright on the moving ride. Ross waved *The Billboard* over our heads.

"I now pronounce you man and wife," he announced as soberly as he could, which was not very sober. "Now let's get on with the damn party!"

Daylight was right around the corner. Our honeymoon consisted of staying in bed until noon and then returning to our regular jobs on the side show. Ann sold tickets. I did the outside bally, then worked my acts inside. There were a lot of throbbing heads around us. Everybody seemed to be walking on tiptoe. The din of the midway pounded louder than ever.

It got to be Fall. I was in my middle thirties, had spent my entire career in traveling show business, and now I was married. We stayed out the season with the carnival, but when it neared its end, we took off. I would soon be a family man; I had just learned that a baby was on the way. No more skylarking around, grabbing a job here and there—anything that would give me a few bucks after my savings from the work season had run out. I needed regular dependable employment that would keep three bodies and three souls together. What was I qualified for?

Civilian life doesn't have many openings for a Human Pin Cushion. I became the night clerk at a hotel not far from the tiny apartment we rented. The job didn't pay much, but it was steady and we made do. Then a crisis arose. It was the kind of crisis only couples living together outside of wedlock and expecting a baby can know: Ann's parents were coming to visit us. You've got to remember this was in the days before such living arrangements had become commonplace. The parents were exceedingly strict religious people and would want to know all about our wedding. They might even want to see our marriage certificate. We talked it over, and with a baby on the way, decided to get married for real.

One of my cousins was pastor of a local church. We went to see him. Could he marry us fast? Ann's parents were due in three days.

"You've got yourself a problem," he said, stating the obvious. "It will take more than three days for the license, blood test, and waiting period."

Our faces fell.

"But I have an idea. Why don't you go to another state?"

It was a great solution, but easier said than done.

"I wish we could," I said. "But we can't even afford to get our car fixed, let alone pay for gas and a hotel out of town."

He puzzled a minute. He got up from his desk and walked around the room. Then he sat down again.

"Here's what I can do," he said. "I'll loan you some money. You can use my secretary's car. I think she'll let you take it if I ask her."

And that's what we did. We drove several miles across the river to the next state, which didn't require waiting, and got formally, legally, and indisputably hitched. Ann's parents arrived in due course and met the side show magician her daughter had definitely married. They were O.K. folks. They didn't flaunt their religion in our faces, and seemed to accept me as a member of the clan. We waved goodbye, really sorry to see them go.

The visit had its aftermath. Ann became homesick to get back to the town where her parents lived. I could understand. It was natural she'd want to give birth with them near. They lived in Florida. We were in the north. It was nearly the end of the off-season, and I knew carnivals would be stirring in the south, so we took off in our rickety automobile, now running again (though just barely), and close to broke as usual, headed out of town. We made it O.K. across two states and hit the bullseye in Georgia. We ran into a carnival routed into Florida. I became a side show hand again, and Ann once more sold tickets. We stayed on the show until it got close to Ann's home town.

There I became the father of a little girl—whom we also named "Ann." "Little Ann," her grandparents called her. To support us, I found a job on a weekly newspaper. I'd been a tramp printer in several off seasons. But I wasn't satisfied with the pay on the weekly, so I nosed around for work on a daily. It turned out there was an opening in another town. The town wasn't far from where Ann's parents lived, so we made the move without too much friction.

There was a car dealership in the new town that was looking for publicity. Apparently, the ad manager of the newspaper told them I'd been a side show magician, and they contacted me. They wanted me to do a "Blindfold Drive." This is the stunt where a blindfold is placed over your eyes, yet you are able to operate a motor car just as if you could see. There's a trick to it, of course. But I did it, at a good price, and the resulting publicity was enormous. It had all taken place in public, with a lot of advance ballyhoo, so everybody in town knew about it.

This included an amateur magician named "John." He got in touch with me, and we spent many hours exchanging magic lore and techniques. One of the things he wanted to know was how I did the Blindfold Drive. I showed him the blindfold I used, which looks opaque enough when it's put on somebody else—so they can verify its "blindness"—but when the man at the wheel (me) puts it on . . . well . . .

I told him it was carried by certain magic shops. He said nothing more about it, so I thought that was the last of it. It wasn't, however. He was part owner of another car dealership, and decided to do the Blindfold Drive himself instead of me, as he had promised. My old wrath came boiling back to me and I cut off all further contact with him.

You might say I had "the last laugh," however. I got hired to do Blindfold Drives at all dealerships in the state that sold the car manufactured by the company whose product I had first publicized. The deal was, we'd have to move to Jacksonville to take advantage of it. I'd be on the road continuously while Ann stayed home and took care of the baby. Ann said we needed the money, so I should do it. We moved to Jacksonville, and I became "Mr. Blindfold Drive" of Florida. Whether John pulled off his version of the same, I never knew.

When that job was over, it was back to my old reliable, the printing trade. Once again, I located an opening on a newspaper. This, of course, was a different newspaper in a different town than my earlier one. But my supple magician's fingers and agile mind again stood me in good stead. When I wasn't distributing type or locking it into forms, I entertained the boys. The boss allowed me to place an ad in the paper for free:

MAGICIAN AVAILABLE for parties, shows, special events. Professional entertainment by ex-Side Show magician. Please phone . . .

It would be part time, of course—probably evenings and weekends because my newspaper job came first. But it produced results. I remember one of the programs in particular. It was a Christmas show for the "Snow Bird Club." This was a bunch of northerners who wintered in Florida. A woman named "Janice" contacted me and said they'd always heard about magicians pulling rabbits out of hats, but never seen one. Could I pull a rabbit out of a hat? Of course I could. Sure.

The truth was, I had never pulled a rabbit out of a hat in my life. In fact, I'd stopped using livestock of any kind long ago. They were too much trouble to carry around, and besides, it cost money to feed them.

But there's a first time for everything, so I located a little white rabbit for the show.

Janice was a joker. She introduced me: "And now, direct from Winter Quarters, where the police are still looking for him . . ." There were chuckles from the crowd. The show went over fine. Then, toward the end, the audience began to laugh—and not at my jokes. They laughed louder and louder. What was happening? Finally, I looked down to see if maybe my fly was open, and saw the little white rabbit peeking out of a coat pocket. I'd stashed it there so I could produce it secretly at the right time.

"Well . . ." I said, "I was asked to do a trick with a rabbit . . . so here he is!"

My face was red, but everybody took it in good spirits and the show, in spite of the bunny boo-boo, was a resounding success. It was followed by the appearance of Santa Claus himself, so there was no break in the merriment. The extra money I made gave us a proper Christmas that year.

I have often thought how that audience of adults behaved like children. But that's Christmas parties, I guess. That's magic.

We had a memorable relationship, Ann and I. We had a lot of adventures together. I remember especially our best home of all: the lovely little cottage we rented back of a kind-hearted lady's house. "Emma" became our good friend, and understood what we meant by "donniker onions" because years ago she'd been a circus performer herself. The "donniker" method of planting anything is simply to cast the seeds on the ground and let them fend for themselves. "Donniker" is circus/carny lingo for "toilet." How that name and the planting idea became connected, I haven't the faintest idea! There were tears when at last we left the cottage and went on the road again.

I worked at countless jobs to keep us going in the off season. I had to. Two more children were born. But when spring came each year, those old feet would start getting itchy, and I'd feel the urge to begin moving again. Ann and the children accompanied me for awhile, but then, our interests having become so separate, they started staying behind, and eventually we made the arrangement permanent.

It was the only parting in my life where I said "goodbye" . . . not "See you down the road."

Was it carnival life or was it me that made it happen? I don't know. I only know I often wake up in the middle of the night troubled and full of anxieties. Sometimes I wonder if they're not really regrets.

16

HOWARD BONE

STEP RIGHT UP!

❧

ODDITIES
OF THE WORLD

Winter Quarters

Admissions – 25 cents
Adults & Children Welcome

When winter winds begin to blow in the northland, circuses and carnivals head south. I shivered on the bally platform. It wasn't exactly winter yet, but I detected a hint of cold weather in the autumn breeze. I'd gotten on a circus side show that played its last dates in southern Michigan, Ohio, Kentucky, Tennessee, and finally Georgia, where it ended its season. Then it headed for winter quarters.

I went with it.

It was kind of a novelty, having a steady show job in the off season. Some carnivals I'd been on worked right through the winter, sticking strictly to the southeast or southwest part of the United States. Some carnivals worked long summer seasons and then broke up for the winter, cutting us all loose to fend for ourselves. I'd pick up with one or another in the spring.

But this was a circus. Its side show went wherever it went. There had been other off-seasons when I'd spent plenty of time in local libraries, mostly to be in a warm place, but in spite of myself, reading a good deal. In a book called *Step Right Up!* I found a pretty accurate description of the difference between a circus and a carnival. Both had side shows, of course. But, as the book said:

> Carnivals are commercial interests; they exist primarily to make money. Also unlike a circus, they are not a show, and they are not meant to be a display of excellence . . . It is a very different kind of entertainment from the circus, which presents us not with illusion but many times with real risk of the performer.

I'd buy that description outright, except the risk in some of my side show acts—like "The Man Who Can't Be Hung"—is plenty real to me. But it's still "illusion," as the book says. There's a trick to it.

These movies that show carnival rides on a circus midway are all wet. No circus in my day offered that kind of diversion. Side shows, yes—carnival rides, no.

Fairgrounds are ideal locations for circus winter quarters. They're usually unused during the hard weather, and they have the barns, stalls, and large arenas circuses need. The circus I was on had rented the fairgrounds near an east coast Florida town, and when the place came up for sale the circus bought it outright. So the circus I was on had its own permanent winter quarters.

I say shows head south. That wasn't always the case. Back in the old days Barnum wintered in Bridgeport, Connecticut; Ringling Bros. wintered in Baraboo, Wisconsin; Hagenbeck-Wallace wintered in Peru, Indiana; and some present-day circuses winter in Missouri and Oklahoma. Not exactly tropical. The change came in the 1920's when "the big one"—Ringling Bros. and Barnum & Bailey—set itself down in Sarasota, Florida, and others followed suit elsewhere in the Sunshine State. Gibsonton, Florida, for instance, is alive with circus people to this day.

My first job in winter quarters was helping repair the big top. Being put up and taken down so often, being raised and lowered in all kinds of weather, it had suffered a genuine beating during the season. I knew the rudiments of sailmaking—I had learned from the best, "Old Dutch," who had been master of a sailing ship—and I'd brought my canvas needles, wax, and a new spool of kite twine with me. The rips and tears were soon sewn up.

Then I was set to checking equipment. The poles and stakes had to be inspected for soundness. The props and rolling stock must be given fresh coats of paint so they'd look bright and sparkling for the next tour. There was side show business to take care of too. I tested the light bulbs we used inside and outside of the show. I made sure there were no dead ones, and no bare spots in the electrical lines. This was actually the job of the circus electrician, but we checked, rechecked, and triple-checked everything. I tried out the bally public address system and made certain all the microphones were in good working order. I got the circus mechanic to go over our trucks as soon as he finished with the kinkers' house trailers. (That's what we called circus performers: "kinkers," as in working the kinks out of sore muscles.)

Paint, repair, replace; those were the main jobs at winter quarters. They occurred over many weeks, so we had ample time to relax and refresh ourselves after the long rigorous season.

As time went on, rehearsals began for the coming shows. Circus acts that stayed on had been practicing their specialties, and the "First-of-Mays"—people new to the circus world—were drifting in. The big top canvas boss put his crew through its paces. The circus riggers readied flying frames, other aerial equipment, and safety nets. The band received sheet music for each act and practiced the sometimes tricky cues. Now came the final days. There were two full-scale rehearsals.

The first rehearsal was simply to make sure everything fell together properly, and timings were right. Is the program routined to best advantage? Would it be better to bring on the jugglers *after* the bear act or *before*? Is the flying trapeze act too long? Does it need to be trimmed? Is there time to set up the net for the Man Shot From A Cannon, or should we have another clown bust-out to get the necessary extra minutes?

The second go was the "dress rehearsal." Like the first rehearsal, it took place in the large fairgrounds building whose arena contained as much area as the big top. The rings were in place and everything was spotted just as it would be on the road. The performers had to be in wardrobe. The band would play its full score. The spotlight operators would be in action. And for the first time, there'd be an audience: side show performers and crew, ticket sellers, cookhouse personnel, big top canvas crew, kinkers until their cue came, visitors from out of town, and the circus owner and his family.

The circus band plays the national anthem. The "Ringmaster" blows his whistle. A new circus show is born.

I played towns and cities that season I can't even remember. Over and over, the marks flocked in, eager to lose themselves for a couple of hours in the wonderland of wire-walkers, tiger trainers, awesome elephants, miraculous flyers, and dazzling bally broads. This time Ann wasn't among them. The side show drew its share of ticket buyers too. Anxious to experience everything, they crowded in to see the "Strange People" —including me, in certain ways the strangest of them all.

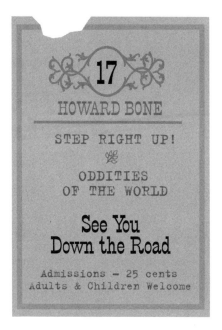

STEP RIGHT UP!

❀

ODDITIES
OF THE WORLD

See You
Down the Road

Admissions – 25 cents
Adults & Children Welcome

T he side show business is the easiest business in the world to quit. I know. I quit it a hundred times. It always pulled me back.

Now I'm retired from the road—and believe me, it's pretty dull.

Pension? Benefits? You've got to be kidding. I can't even afford to take the daily newspaper. A telephone? Don't make me laugh.

But forgive me. I'm not complaining. These are just facts. Still, I can't help but look back on my life and wonder what it all added up to. A marriage that ended in divorce. Children who are out there somewhere. A string of performances probably forgotten by the thousands upon thousands who witnessed them. I can no longer bend my thumbs enough to get out of regulation police handcuffs. I once could—never used a hidden key. My fingers are too arthritic to make a fan of cards, even with my own deck. The V.A. says my ticker isn't what it ought to be.

A fine ending for *The World's Greatest Magician.*

But somehow, there's something inside me that won't go away. Just the other day, I consulted a Rand McNally atlas in the library to find out where a certain tall-grass town was located. I'd read that a carnival was playing there, and for a moment I considered trying to land a job on it. No car, no bus money. I'd have to hitchhike or catch a ride in a railroad box car, if they still exist. Eat? Sleep? It would have to be in the nearest Salvation Army lodge or rescue mission. Or maybe sleep under a bridge or highway overpass.

Well . . . it was a passing fancy.

But I've saved out fifty cents from the grocery money. It only means a few more peanut butter sandwich suppers. I keep the coins in an empty pill box by my bed. I want to be ready to buy the Route Card for the next carnival I'm on . . . should the occasion arise, of course.

I wonder what the route will be?

GLOSSARY

Like many other specialized pursuits, the circus and carnival worlds have their own jargon. It is perfectly well understood by those who are with it, but something of a mystery to outsiders. Demystification of a few selected terms follows:

At' Show   An "Athletic Show." A midway attraction, not an Olympic event. "At' Shows" are described within Howard Bone's story.

Back door   Entrance into the big top for performers.

Bally   as in "Ballyhoo." A multi-purpose term, it is used to refer to the come-on spiel of the "talker," the raised platform outside the side show entrance, and free shows there.

Bally Broads   "Bally," in this case, is a corruption of the word "Ballet." The term is circus jargon for the show girls whose main function is to look beautiful and lend color and glamour to the show. They are all-around, though unfeatured, performers, working on the ground, on elephants, in the air, and with numerous costume changes, wherever they're needed.

Bannerline The lineup of large canvas banners in front of the side show tent. They are painted with florid representations of the wonders to be seen within. To say most of these are highly imaginative is putting it mildly. They are usually downright exaggerated, misleading, and false. Their purpose is to stir onlookers to buy tickets and in this they certainly succeed. Their "folk art" appeal has made them sought after by collectors.

Billboard Wedding The carny blessing is the union of two people in a special ceremony. *The Billboard* magazine is waved over the heads of the happy couple as they are pronounced "Man and Wife." It is usually a gala occasion, the same as a regulation wedding, although without benefit of clergy.

Blindfold Drive Driver of a motor car is blindfolded but still able to pilot the machine as well as if the eyes were clear. Usually a publicity stunt, it draws throngs of spectators. It generally ends up at the business that sponsors it, or the carnival, circus, or fair that stages it. Since it falls into the category of a magic trick it is also a potent promotion for traveling magic shows.

Bull Elephant of either sex. A "Railroad Bull" is not a pachyderm but a detective or "security" man in railroad employ. Their tendency to strong-arm tactics and gun slinging became legendary.

Bull hook A short-handled tool with a metal "hook" on the end, used to guide and control elephants. It is not as vicious as it sounds.

Bust out Refers to a whole flock of clowns "busting out" of the back door and into the rings.

Candy Butcher A person who sells candy and other refreshments, usually during a performance, and usually circulating through the audience to do so. They're the people who sometimes get in your way when you're trying to see some breathtaking moment in the ring.

Carny Short for "Carnival Worker." Anyone who's on a carnival.

Concessions Booths on carnivals offering such things as games of chance, weight guessing, souvenirs, and the like. They're run by "Concessionaires."

Donniker On a circus or carnival you never refer to a "toilet," "lavatory," or "rest room." It's the "donniker." (Also sometimes "doniker," or "donnicker.")

Gazonie Lowest form of life on a carnival. Usually applied to itinerant carny laborers who are frequently winos, junkies, fugitives on the run, and those who are prone to violence, thievery, and anti-social behavior. It is not unusual to find mental defectives among them. Gazonies come and go with frequency.

Grease Joint Hamburger stand or any stand where food is sold to the "marks" (which see) on carnival lots.

Hey Rube! The old time cry of carnival or circus people to call for help during a major fracas. It tended to galvanize every showhand on the lot. Tent stakes were a favorite weapon. In Howard Bone's day "Hey Rube!" had been replaced with "Signal 25" over a loudspeaker.

Hippodrome or "Hippodrome track." Simply the wide pathway that runs around the arena, outside the circus rings. The "spec" parades on this track.

Jackpots You "cut up" jackpots—sometimes shortened to "jackies." Jackpots are gab sessions among troupers: gossip, yarns, news of happenings to people and shows, tales of years gone by . . . to name a few "jackpot" topics. The civilian equivalent is the kind of verbal exchange that used to go on in barbershops or around pot-bellied stoves in country stores.

Lecture The spoken lines delivered by the "Lecturer" inside the side show tent as he presents the wonders therein. Not to be confused with "lectures" as understood on college campuses.

Mark or "Marks." The customers of carnivals or circuses, members of the ticket buying public. One story of its origin involves carnies secretly putting a chalk mark on the back of a customer's jacket to indicate a gullible person, ripe for a con.

On   If you are employed by a carnival or circus, you are not "in" it, you are "on" it.

Pie Car   or "Pie Wagon." On railroad shows, the equivalent of a dining car, although much less grand. Generally open 24 hours a day for food, coffee, and, when possible, hard liquor, it's traditionally a good place to gather and cut up jackpots. Non-railroad shows have the equivalent.

Possum Belly Queen   A term given to a town girl who thinks she has fallen in love with a carny. The name comes from the "possum belly" of certain carnival semis, where there is a compartment added underneath to hold shown equipment. The space, when empty, makes a handy hideaway for the two lovebirds.

Punk   Artificial freak, made of rubber or some pliable substance, intended to be displayed in a formaldehyde-filled jar. Examples would be two-headed babies, foetuses, heads of famous criminals, or other body parts with malformations. The list of punks is long. They look real but are not.

Route Card   A printed card or sheet showing the lineup of towns to be played during the season—or as far ahead as the show is booked. Like most everything else provided by management, they are not free. In Howard Bone's day they cost fifty cents. Show personnel like them because, among other things, they forecast where mail should be sent.

Signal 25   See "Hey Rube!"

Spec   A spectacular parade around the hippodrome track, usually at the beginning, sometimes at points within the show, and often at the end. The classic "spec" consists of imaginatively garbed performers, clowns, elaborate floats, beautiful showgirls, animals, and, generally at the end, colorfully blanketed elephants. Due to their cost, today's "specs" are hardly spectacular at all, but simply a walk-around of people who'll be performing in the show. The true "spec" has an overall theme, such as "Mother Goose," "Hollywood," or "Old Glory."   One of the all-time great "specs" was called "Lalla Rookh" and boggled the mind with its visions of sumptuous oriental splendor.

Straw House   The tented show-business term for a totally full house. In the old days, straw was strewn on the ground so the audience overflow would have a place to sit. "Straw House" is the equivalent of the theatre's "S.R.O."—"Standing Room Only."

Talker   Known to the public as a "barker," he stands on the bally platform (or at the ticket box) outside the tent and talks up the attractions to be seen inside. His spiel is usually a masterpiece of psychology. Some "talkers" get a percentage of tickets they succeed in selling.

Tip   The crowd drawn to the spiel of the "Talker." Also, the portion of that crowd that buys tickets and comes in to see the show. "A good tip" means a good-sized audience.

Top   "Tent" to outsiders. In circuses, the term is used for any canvas structure. The "Big Top" is where the main circus performance takes place. "The side show top," the "Horse Top," the "Cookhouse Top," and the "Menagerie Top" are other examples of the word's use. It appears to be less used in carnivals.

With it   If you're "with it" you are an insider in the world of outdoor show business. It not only means you work on a carnival or circus, but implies a kind of spiritual affinity.

PUBLICATIONS YOU MAY ENJOY READING

Freak Show
by Carl Hammer and Gideon Bosker
Chronicle Books, 1996.
85 Second St.
San Francisco, CA   94105

James Taylor's Shocked and Amazed!
by James Taylor
Dolphin-Moon Press
Atomic Books
229 West Read St.
Baltimore, MD   21201

Jay's Journal of Anomalies
by Ricky Jay
Farrar, Straus & Giroux, 2001.
19 Union Square West
New York, NY   10003

Step Right Up!
by LaVahn G. Hoh & William H. Rough
Betterway Publications, Inc., 1990.
P.O. Box 219
Crozet, VA   22932

When I'm Dead All This Will Be Yours
Joe Teller: A Portrait By His Kid
by Teller
Blast Books, Inc., 2000.
P.O. Box 51, Cooper Station
New York, NY   10276-0051

BOOKS BY SUN DOG PRESS

STEVE RICHMOND, *Santa Monica Poems*

STEVE RICHMOND, *Hitler Painted Roses*
(Foreword by Charles Bukowski)

STEVE RICHMOND, *Spinning Off Bukowski*

NEELI CHERKOVSKI, *Elegy for Bob Kaufman*

RANDALL GARRISON, *Lust in America*

BILLY CHILDISH, *Notebooks of a Naked Youth*

DAN FANTE, *Chump Change*

ROBERT STEVEN RHINE, *My Brain Escapes Me*

FERNANDA PIVANO, *Charles Bukowski: Laughing
With the Gods*

JEAN-FRANCOIS DUVAL, *Bukowski and the Beats*

Printed for Sun Dog Press, 2001.
The text is set in Adobe Jenson.